Praise for *Missing Jesus*

"Our passion as hymn writers is to serve the church with songs that draw people into deeper fellowship with Jesus Christ. The body of Christ needs this desperately, not only in music but also in print. *Missing Jesus* has been long in the making and was written for this purpose. We are thrilled to finally see it in print!"

— **KEITH AND KRISTYN GETTY, recording artists and writers of *In Christ Alone***

"One of my favorite scriptures is 'your life is now hidden with Christ in God.' Oh, friend, we will never know who we truly are apart from Christ—and Charles and Janet Morris in their new book, *Missing Jesus*, unfold the beauty of knowing our Savior at the deepest level. Only in him do we understand our own story, and I thank my good friends Charles and Janet for helping us apprehend the graciousness and loveliness of Jesus."

— **JONI EARECKSON TADA, bestselling author and founder of Joni and Friends International Disability Center**

"The Morrises see that many professed Christians actually keep Christ at a distance, to their own loss. But the stories told here, vivid, poignant, and searching as they are, should bring him and us close."

— **J. I. PACKER, professor of theology at Regent College and author of *Knowing God***

"Charles and Janet have written an encouraging book. And the Lord knows we need encouragement! Their gentle pursuit of a grace-filled life will reorient your soul. This book will not only warm your heart but brace you for the chill of a post-Christian world."

— **PAUL MILLER, author of *A Praying Life***

"What a wonderful book . . . I read it in three sittings and did not want to put it down. *Missing Jesus* draws me back to a daily personal relationship with Jesus."

—**JONATHAN FRANK,** *HAVEN Today* **listener**

"For too many years I thought that the storyline of the Bible was primarily about me—at first about how I could get what I wanted, and then later about how I was doing on the road of my personal transformation. And then Jesus showed up and began to teach me that he is the Story, that he is the subject of all the verbs. *Missing Jesus* is a book where you will find him, and in the most surprising yet ordinary places: at a graveside, on a dirt road, in the cracking of a crust of bread. I love this book and wholeheartedly recommend it."

—**ELYSE FITZPATRICK, author of** *Found in Him: The Joy of the Incarnation and Our Union with Christ*

"How strange we humans are! Even as Christians we will latch on to anything at all for stability and meaning, while sidelining Christ himself. We must be constantly brought back to the living heart of the gospel, Jesus himself. *Missing Jesus* is surefooted shepherding to get us there."

—**DANE ORTLUND, PhD, senior vice president, Bible Publishing, Crossway**

MISSING JESUS

Find Your
Life in His
Great Story

CHARLES & JANET MORRIS

FOREWORD BY ANN VOSKAMP

MOODY PUBLISHERS
CHICAGO

All Scripture quotation, unless otherwise indicated, are taken from the Holy Bible, New International Version®, NIV®. Copyright © 1973, 1978, 1984, 2011 by Biblica, Inc.™ Used by permission of Zondervan. All rights reserved worldwide. www.zondervan.com. The "NIV" and "New International Version" are trademarks registered in the United States Patent and Trademark Office by Biblica, Inc.™

Scripture quotations marked NLT are taken from the *Holy Bible, New Living Translation,* copyright © 1996, 2004. Used by permission of Tyndale House Publishers, Inc., Wheaton Illinois 60189, U.S.A. All rights reserved.

Scripture quotations marked NASB are taken from the *New American Standard Bible*®, Copyright © 1960, 1962, 1963, 1968, 1971, 1972, 1973, 1975, 1977, 1995 by The Lockman Foundation. Used by permission. (www.Lockman.org)

Scripture quotations marked NKJV are taken from the *New King James Version.* Copyright © 1982 by Thomas Nelson, Inc. Used by permission. All rights reserved.

Scripture quotations marked NEB are taken from *The New English Bible.* Copyright © 1961 by Oxford University Press and Cambridge University Press. Used by permission.

Scripture quotations marked PHILLIPS are taken from *The New Testament in Modern English* by J. B. Phillips © HarperCollins and J. B. Phillips 1958, 1960, 1972.

Edited by Elizabeth Cody Newenhuyse
Interior and cover design: Erik M. Peterson
Cover photo of waterfall copyright © 2013 by Offset/Peter Adams. All rights reserved
Author photos: Bill Blakey.

\
ISBN: 978-0-8024-1128-0

We hope you enjoy this book from Moody Publishers. Our goal is to provide high-quality, thought-provoking books and products that connect truth to your real needs and challenges. For more information on other books and products written and produced from a biblical perspective, go to www.moodypublishers.com or write to:

Moody Publishers
820 N. LaSalle Boulevard
Chicago, IL 60610

1 3 5 7 9 10 8 6 4 2

Printed in the United States of America

*"The sun of righteousness will rise with healing in its rays.
And you will go out and frolic like well-fed calves."*
(Malachi 4:2)

Contents

Foreword

*M*issing Jesus has been by my bedside stand since Charles and Janet sent it my way. I have been deeply ministered to by reading it. This precious couple have a heart after Christ's that is such a joy, such a testament, such a deep encouragement to this world. I believe their ministry is anointed of God for such a time as this. I have been praying that the needful and necessary work of *Missing Jesus* goes out into the world and blesses so many hungry, hurting hearts. You will find powerful stories here—God stories—every word glowing with what we all need: grace. Grace pulses through every line of this refreshing book and will lead your weary heart closer to Jesus. Nothing matters more than this.

Sometimes that feeling that we're missing *something*—is because we are really missing *Someone*. Nothing aches like missing Jesus.

Every page of this needed book welcomes you closer into his heart again. Nothing could be better than this.

I thank Jesus when Charles and Janet come to mind, for they and their ministry have very personally changed my life. Their hearts beat together in exalting Jesus in all things. These friends bring great joy to me. I truly loved reading this book and believe that through *Missing Jesus*, they will bring great joy to you too.

—ANN VOSKAMP
Farmer's wife, mother to six, author of the *New York Times* bestseller *One Thousand Gifts: A Dare to Live Fully Right Where You Are*

What's in It for Me?

What makes us decide to read a book? Analysts say we're always asking one simple question: "What's in it for me?" Is it going to entertain me? Will it fill a gap in my knowledge? Does it meet a pressing need? If the answer is yes, then we're likely to read it. A friend of ours just had a heart attack, and the day he left the hospital he was looking for a book to help him with his recovery. Sometimes we need some concrete, problem-focused help. Sometimes we need a good story. Sometimes we need some information. Those are all good things.

What we don't need is another book that says, "It's All about You." We've already read that one. We really have. It's the world we live in all the time, the one where we're solidly at the center and everything revolves around us. It's the message that comes at us from every direction: marketers sell us secrets to success; educators fuel our self-esteem; self-help gurus pump us up with possibilities. One simple, unspoken theme runs through it all: It's all about you. This may sound like good news, but it's actually bad news because it turns us back on ourselves. We end up in the selfsame place we were in when we started.

What we need is to be redirected, away from ourselves onto something much more massive and glorious. That's what changes everything, that's what sets us free, and the good news is—that's what God has given us in Jesus. It's good news because we're not big enough to be the center of our own lives. We're like the solar system without the sun. The sun is so massive it can hold all the planets in their orbits, but we're not the sun. We simply don't have the gravity to hold our lives together even when we expend a lot of effort trying. What we need is the good news of Jesus Christ, the good news that we can look outside ourselves at last because God has provided everything we need in Jesus. God has sent his glorious Son into the world to be everything for us, to be the center of our lives, to draw us into fellowship with the living God. And it's all by grace. None of it is up to us.

As believers we need to keep on hearing this good news over and over again because we have a great tendency to lose sight of Jesus. At first he fills the horizons of our lives but after a while he can fade off into the periphery. We asked our coworker David Wollen how he'd sum up the problem most of us have as believers and his answer was simple but profound: "We feel like we're missing something, and we probably are. We're probably missing Jesus."

That's what this book is about—it's about not missing Jesus. It's about seeing him big. It's about having our lives re-centered on the glorious Son of God all over again—because that's what sets us free.

—CHARLES AND JANET MORRIS

Part 1

SEEING HIM BIG

Who Is Worthy of My Life?

The scent of curry wafted out of Mr. Gupta's restaurant, saris filled the shop next door, and down the road we could just see the corner of a Hindu temple. It might have been Calcutta except for the red double-decker buses passing by. We were in London on a short-term mission trip with about forty other people. The first few days we'd walked around this South Asian neighborhood, imbibing the culture, occasionally gathering to pray, but now it was time to move on to the hard stuff, to hand out tracts and start some conversations. We had come here to share the good news of God's redemption—to shine the light of the cross. The glory of that vision had packed our bags and walked us on to the plane, but now that we were here, it had somehow shrunk down and then—poof—disappeared. The drizzle was hastening the footsteps of the people passing by. No one seemed inclined to talk. All we could see was the God-excluding world going about its business and we were left wondering what in the world we were doing out on a sidewalk five thousand miles from home.

That's what happens when we lose sight of Jesus. Life gets small. The horizons of our hearts close in, the world shrinks down, and the glory departs. I (Charles) speak five days a week on the radio about Jesus, and Janet helps write the programs. You'd think two people like us who spend so many hours studying and talking and writing about Jesus would be filled with his glory all the time but . . . no. We can miss Jesus.

Before I arrived as the fourth host for this eighty-year-old Christian radio program, Janet and I were living our dream life. I've worked a lot of jobs—reporter, press secretary, bureau chief for United Press International—but at this point I was a freelance consultant for several Christian ministries. My life included plenty of airports but much of the time I could work from home, sipping fresh-ground coffee in our mountain home nine thousand feet above sea level. The seasons would change from aspen gold to a snow-clad winter. A purple lupine–decked spring would usher in a perfect Rocky Mountain summer. We live in a culture that tells us to pursue our dreams and for us this was it. And yet, it felt a little stale, a little insulated and isolated—a little small. We wanted the excitement of living all-out for Jesus and one day we made it a prayer. We told the Lord we were willing to go anywhere he wanted us to go—with one small stipulation. "Please, Lord. Don't send us to Southern California." I can remember telling Janet, "We've moved to a lot of different places over the years but at least I've never asked you to move to Southern California." We pictured it as a hot, overcrowded, smog-choked, twelve-lane freeway built right on top the San Andreas Fault. "Africa maybe, Lord, but not Southern California."

A few days later the call came from Haven Ministries asking me to become the new host, and no, I couldn't do it from the Rocky Mountains; we had to relocate.

You guessed it. Six months later we were driving down that twelve-lane freeway pulling a U-Haul.

> *I can talk every day on the radio and still lose sight of Jesus.*

Thirteen years later we've become typical Southern Californians who brag about the weather and enjoy the thrill of a little tremor now and then, but at the time it felt a little like we were dying for Jesus. I thought it would lock him into my heart for life but I soon found out it doesn't work that way. I can talk every day on the radio and still lose sight of Jesus. I can get caught up in the regret of not having a fat 401(k). I can find myself coveting my friend's fully restored British-racing-green MGB convertible. There's that jealousy I feel when I hear a better preacher on the radio, the longing for trips I may never get to take, the worry over my health, the newest electronic toy I can't live without. My life can even shrink down to the next slice of cherry pie I'm going to eat or whether or not tonight's NCIS is one I've seen before.

I can live small—and when I do I reduce Jesus. An author we read recently called Jesus her "little glow light" and I can start to treat the crucified Son of God like it's all about me, and he's just an accessory who adds a little glow to my existence. I can consign him to the margins of my life while I pursue my own agenda. The shadows can block my heart so I don't comprehend the magnitude of his love or the absolute completeness of his grace. I need to see his glory—again and again. We all do. We need him to break into our hearts and fill us with a fresh realization of who he is and what he's done for us so we can live large, liberated lives.

We needed Jesus to break into our hearts the day we were out on that rainy sidewalk in London and he did, right then and there, in a way we didn't expect. A young West Asian woman slowed down, took one of our tracts, and paused as she read the title, "Have You Ever Wanted a New Life?"

Janet said, "It's about Jesus. Do you know about Jesus?"

"Not much," she said, "but I've been looking for someone who's worthy of my life."

"Well, that would definitely be Jesus," Janet told her.

She nodded her thanks and began reading as she went on her way, leaving us to marvel that someone who didn't even know him would use that biblical word *worthy*. We rolled it around in our hearts. Who is worthy of our lives? Who but Jesus? According to the Bible, the entire universe is singing "worthy" to him and that young woman's comment made it real to us again. He is the only one who is worthy, not only of our lives, but of everything in all of creation. It was like waking from a trance.

We need to wake from that trance. We need his glory to keep on breaking into our hearts and waking us up, because when we see his glory it changes everything.

I suspect the apostle John needed Jesus to break in on him again. He'd been exiled to the island of Patmos for refusing to worship the Roman emperor. I can imagine him sitting there all alone, an old man, listening to the crash of the waves and the cry of the gulls, needing to see Jesus. Suddenly it happened. An angel appeared in that unrelenting blue expanse of Mediterranean sky and John saw a door opened wide to reveal the heartbeat truth of the universe—a Lamb standing in the middle of a throne, looking as if it had been slain, with everything in all creation worshiping and crying out, "Worthy is the Lamb, who was slain, to receive power and wealth and wisdom and strength and honor and glory and praise!"

That revelation broke right into John's world, into the apparent dominance of Roman power, into the seeming weakness of Christ's church, into his own lonely isolation, and it showed him what was true—that the Father has lifted up the crucified Lamb, the one who was lifted up for us, and placed him on the throne of the world. Anyone who wants to know what life is all about can just look through that door and see the answer—it's all about Jesus. He has all the mass, all the gravity, all the authority, and all the right to all the worship from all of creation for all eternity—all because he offered himself as a sacrificial lamb for the redemption of the world. That's what we need to see. We need the Lamb on the throne to break through to us again and again and deliver us out of our small way of life.

That wet day in London he possibly broke through to a young West Asian woman, because who else could have planted such high expectations and such an intentional quest in her heart but Jesus? To this day Janet and I marvel at the wisdom of her words, because who understands that we're meant to give our lives away? Our culture is constantly telling us "it's all about you" and sending us headlong after our own self-centered pursuits. Our grasping and gripping fuels the fallen world. We're all trying to make lives for ourselves and yet we end up giving our lives away in the process. I suspect most of the people hurrying down the sidewalk that day were giving themselves away without realizing they were doing it. They were squandering themselves on goals and desires that have no more ultimate

Anyone who wants to know what life is all about can just look through that door.

value than those little Hindu statuettes down the road that were so clearly unworthy of the devotion they were receiving.

We'd visited that Hindu temple the day before and it seemed incredible that people—living, breathing images of God—would offer themselves up to dead images staring lifelessly out of eyes that can't see, with mouths that can't speak. We even saw a father gently remove his little daughter's shoes and give her a bunch of flowers to carry in and offer to the gilded things lined up against the wall. It was heart wrenching.

But the idols aren't just in the temples; there's a vast array of unworthy gods making a claim on our lives. We each have our own personal collection and the media is always offering up a fresh supply. Living in Southern California is like living in a state of denial where the good life is always on display, the sun always shines, no one gets old, the roses bloom in January, and the malls are full of sparkling new possibilities you can bring home in a bag. The world is presenting this illusion to us all the time regardless of where we live. The idols are always making promises and then failing to deliver.

The Lamb is different. The idols require our sacrifices and still withhold their blessings, but the Lamb, he doesn't make demands; he fulfills them. He doesn't squeeze out our lifeblood; he pours his out for us. He gave himself so we could be liberated and enriched beyond our comprehension, so the floodgates of blessing could be opened up wide. As believers we need to realize this again and again. We need to see the glory of the One we were created to worship. We need an ongoing Copernican revolution in our hearts.

A s Janet and I pondered how to convey the difference it makes in our lives to see the glory of Jesus, we thought of Copernicus. In the sixteenth century the prevailing assumption was that the earth was the center of the cosmos and that the sun revolved around the earth. Then Copernicus came along and demonstrated that, despite appearances, it's actually the other way around. It's the earth that revolves around the sun.

We need to see this. From our terra firma point of view we naturally live as if we're the dead center of everything and everything revolves around us. We get trapped in this "all about me" mentality, this effort to pull in the good things we think we want. We end up spinning in circles, exhausting ourselves with the sheer effort of managing our own existence. We need a Copernican revolution, a simple but profound shift in our worldview that comes from seeing the crucified, resurrected Jesus on the throne of the cosmos and realizing that he is at the center of creation and that he is everything we could possibly ever want or need. It's a simple shift in perspective but it changes everything. It transforms our small, self-centered world into the glorious "all about Jesus" universe where he reigns in the glory of his grace.

Eugene Peterson says that "Failure to worship consigns us to a life of spasms and jerks, at the mercy of every advertisement, every seduction, every siren. . . . People who do not worship are swept into a vast restlessness, epidemic in the world, with no steady direction and no sustaining purpose."[1] Even as believers we can live that way, with no steady direction and no sustaining purpose. We need a regular shift away from ourselves to the One who truly is at the center of everything so we can live a life of unfettered, worshipful joy. We need him to draw us out of our self-circling way of life and orient us to himself and to his glory.

A few years back, our friend Darrell Johnson told us about the personal Copernican revolution he had as a college student. He'd been a rising star, a brain, a promising physicist with a potential scholarship to study in Europe and a professor/mentor who was helping him chart his course. He'd been a believer for most of his young life but a fresh new love for Jesus had come pouring into his heart and with it came a call to preach the gospel. How do you switch paths when you're being carried along by all kinds of bright prospects and gifts you feel compelled to use? How do you face the people who won't understand and will surely be disappointed? When Darrell sat in his professor's office and told him what he was thinking of doing, the response was exactly what you'd expect it to be, "Why would you throw your brains and your promising future away to preach Jesus?"

This was back in the late sixties when *Jesus Christ Superstar* was the big hit. The title song was being played constantly on the radio. "Jesus Christ, Superstar, do you think you're who they say you are?" As Darrell listened to those lyrics it came to him that this was the crucial question—who does Jesus say he is? If Jesus was going to outweigh everything else in life, it wasn't enough to know what other people had to say about him. Darrell needed him to speak his glory directly and personally into his heart. So he asked him—"Jesus, who do you say you are?"

He started reading the gospel of John for an answer and when he came to chapter 8 he slowed down as if he was treading on holy ground. Right there on the pages of his Bible was the very same question he'd been asking. The buzz about Jesus had reached a high pitch. Everyone was speculating and arguing about who this new rabbi might actually be. The people of his own day were asking Jesus, "Who are you?" Without any fanfare, Jesus spoke words that startled everyone. "When you have lifted up the Son of Man, then you will know that I AM." "I tell you the truth, before Abraham was born, I AM."

He said those words during the Feast of the Tabernacles when the people had come to Jerusalem filled with expectation that the Messiah was going to arrive at any moment and usher in a new age. The temple courts had been lit up every night with great lights symbolizing the brilliant supernatural light they believed was about to dawn on the world. It was in that context that Jesus told them, "I AM the Light of the World," not just one of many lights, but the only light, the only way out of darkness for the entire world. Needless to say he raised some hackles but what made his statement even more outrageous to his Jewish listeners were those words, "I AM," in Greek "ego eimi," which literally mean, "I, I am" or "I am who I am." They come straight out of God's revelation to Moses in the wilderness. Moses asked the Lord what to tell the Israelites when they wanted to know his name and the answer came back, "Tell them, 'I Am Who I AM.'" Was Jesus actually claiming to be not just the Messiah, not just the light of the world, but the Lord of the burning bush?

That's what the religious leaders wanted to know. They wanted him to either back down or condemn himself so they pressed him hard with more questions. Jesus didn't back down. He told them plainly that they would die in their sins unless they believed that he was the One he claimed to be. The leaders understood the implications and they were ready to kill him for it.

The world we live in is not much different. John wrote his gospel in the midst of a pagan world where gaining "light" was a universal spiritual concern. It's the same today. People are groping in the darkness and our Western world has turned East for spiritual answers. Buddha supposedly once said, "If you see the Buddha in the road, shoot him." A Buddhist-leaning friend of ours explained that this is a warning not to let anyone intrude himself into your search for spiritual light. Everything has to be cleared away, every thought, every person, every preconceived notion, so you can find your own way. We're being told this in one form or another all the time. This same spiritual message is being woven all through our culture and it never challenges our centrality; it only reinforces it.

Jesus does just the opposite. He puts himself squarely in our road and points to himself and says, "Look to me. I am the light of the world." The world is telling us we have a divine spark within us; that we just need to be true to ourselves. It's flattering but we need to be clear that Jesus is flatly contradicting this assertion and all the spiritual systems that teach it. He says that, to the contrary, we're actually filled with deep darkness. We need the light to shine into our hearts and bring us to life and he is that light. The pluralistic world doesn't want to hear this message but there wasn't a hateful bone in Jesus' body when he said it, only love willing to affront our pride so we could be saved.

Jesus is not one of many lights. Jesus is the Sun. When we see his cosmic significance it reorders our world. The weight of his glory starts to outweigh everything else. It delivers us out of our small way of life into a wide and joyous orbit of worship.

You've no doubt guessed the road Darrell decided to take. He knew Jesus had answered his question. The weight of Jesus' words gave him the sheer chutzpah he needed to change his course. His professor friend was worried he was wasting his life but Darrell knew better. He'd heard Jesus say, "I AM." He'd watched him go to the cross and rise again. He knew Jesus was on the throne of the world, that he was worthy, and that there was nothing to fear and everything to gain if he gave his life for him.

We heard Darrell tell this story in a sermon he preached many decades later where he actually sang "Jesus Christ Superstar" from the pulpit. We've also taken a two-week course he taught on the gospel of John where he showed how John states his theme right up front in his gospel when he says, "We have seen his glory, the glory of the one and only Son," and then starts unfolding the glory of Jesus so we can see it too. We see him turn water into wine, heal a crippled man, feed a huge throng of hungry people, even walk on water. We hear his brilliant repartee with the religious leaders and his compassionate love for those who come to him in need. His personality emerges right out of the pages of the Bible but as Darrell pointed out, none of these things fully communicates the glory of Jesus. The turning point comes in chapter 12 when he cries out, "The hour has come for the Son of Man to be glorified." It was a gut-wrenching cry that must have come from the depths of his heart because the hour he was talking about was the hour of his sacrifice. He knew that he was about to go to the cross and that it would be right there in those hours of suffering and shame, in that singular act of love, that his glory would be fully revealed.

We have a tendency to miss the cross once we come to faith. We can treat it like the key that gets us in the door and then gets tossed aside as we go on to other things. If Jesus has lost his central place in our lives it's probably because we've left the cross behind. We need to continually fill up on the glory of his death, to keep taking in the sheer breathtaking wonder of the Son of God stretched out in love and nailed onto those rough wooden beams.

The cross is not a little thing we wear around our necks; it's the glory of God revealed, the glory of his love, the centerpiece of all creation. Jesus said that when he was lifted up he would draw all men to himself. It's the cross that draws us when we first come to faith and it's meant to keep on drawing us. We need it to preach the gospel to our hearts again and again because one of the reasons we live small is that we feel guilty. The Bible says people "repress the knowledge of God," but it's not just unbelievers who do that. We can do it ourselves. We know we're meant to live all-out for Jesus and when we don't our guilt sends us into God-avoidance. We think he's keeping us at arm's length and making demands that we can't keep. He feels a million miles away and the cross is the only thing that can draw us back into his gravitational field. That's where we see him as he truly is, not the way our darkened hearts imagine him to be. That's where he opens up the very depths of his own heart so we can understand that he's not trying to keep us away; he's drawing us in. He let his body be broken and his blood be shed so he could have us close to him.

We need to take this in every day. There's nothing keeping us away from Jesus because his death tore through the barriers. All the dark clouds of anger have disappeared. We don't have to stay in our lonely planet way of life because Jesus removed every shred of our guilt forever. He's drawing us into a fellowship of love where he gives us everything, grace upon grace, all wrapped up in himself, and we can just take it—and then give ourselves to him in return. That's how it's meant to work. Paul summed it up in 2 Corinthians 5:15: "He died for all, that those who live should no longer live for themselves but for him who died for them and was raised again."

Note

1. Eugene Peterson, *Reversed Thunder* (HarperSanFrancisco, 1988), 60.

2

Living in
the Great Story

The door opens. John sees someone sitting on a throne holding a scroll. A question rings out, "Who is worthy to open the scroll?" Then the answer comes back, "no one," and John weeps and weeps as if his heart would break.

Then one of the elders consoles him with joyous news: "Do not weep! See, the Lion of the tribe of Judah, the Root of David, has triumphed. He is able to open the scroll and its seven seals."

That's when John sees the Lamb on the throne looking as if it had been slain. That's when the crowd starts to sing, "Worthy is the Lamb, who was slain, to receive power and wealth and wisdom and strength and honor and glory and praise!"

We just walked in on a story. In fact, we've come in at the climax, the turning point, the moment of resolution that comes in every good story; only this isn't just any story, this is the true tale of creation itself. This is the story of God and his world, the story of the great triumph of his love. This is the true narrative of our lives, the one that delivers us out of that small story where everything revolves around us.

We need to lean hard on God's shoulder and listen with all of our hearts as he tells us the grand drama of the world's redemption. He'll take us back to the genesis of every tear when the earth swung out of its orbit and we were wrenched out of life. He'll open up the great dilemma of the fallen world that runs through the entire Bible and begs for an answer. He'll make us understand the depth of the problem and what's at stake and take us through the rises and falls of hope so—when the answer finally comes—we'll be able to join the choir of the universe. When we hear him say, "Do not weep! See, the Lion of the Tribe of Judah, the Root of David, has triumphed," we won't be yawning. We'll understand why this is the best news the world has ever heard. We'll understand that life has meaning after all and that this is it—right here—this Lamb on the throne.

Ann Voskamp tells in her blog how her youngest son was totally drawn into the story of Joseph when she read it aloud from Genesis. By the time she got to where the steward planted a silver chalice to incriminate the youngest brother, her little boy was leaning hard on her shoulder. When she read the fatal words, "And the cup was found in Benjamin's sack," he burst into tears.

Ann said she couldn't leave her youngest hanging in grief. She had to read on because "it's knowing the end of the story that wipes away the tears."[1] She had to keep going until Joseph revealed himself to his brothers and reassured them that, while they had meant their treachery for evil, "God meant it for good." But that was just a preview ending, a foretaste of a greater ending still to come. God saves the day through Joseph but there's another installment coming and then another and another. The story keeps unrolling like a red carpet until it finally stops at the feet of Jesus—who really and truly saves the day.

Charles Dickens used to release his novels chapter by chapter. Each chapter was like a little magazine and when the last one was released people would bind them together as a book. When "The Old Curiosity Shop" was coming out the anticipation was so great the crowds stood on the docks in New York waiting for the next installment to arrive from England. As the gangplank was lowered they yelled to the crew, "Is little Nell dead?" God's story comes in installments, too. The events in the Bible are all part of God's deeply engaging plan to redeem his world, all moving forward to a final conclusion, one installment at a time. He wants us to read it with great anticipation, to be so invested we're tempted to yell, "Is the world dead yet?" and hope with all of our hearts that it isn't so. Dickens admitted he didn't always know where his story was going, but God always does. He wants us to see how intricately he's woven it together, how it was always heading for his final glorious installment—how it was always all about Jesus.

When we miss that, when we don't see that the Bible is all about Jesus, we end up losing the thread of the story. I (Charles) grew up in Kansas, North Dakota, Louisiana, Oklahoma, wherever my dad's oil company job took us, and we always went to church. There were Sunday school lessons and vacation Bible schools and those stories my mother would read to me at night. They challenged me to dare to be a Daniel, to be strong like Samson, to take on my Goliaths like David. Of course I was told that I was born into sin and that my sins kept me apart from God but those Old Testament heroes kept reminding me that I was expected to be good.

The truth is— the more of him, the more of us.

Finally at the age of sixteen during one long night of struggle, the good news took root in my heart. After listening to a young preacher talk about the cross I went home in turmoil. I was driven to the gospel of John and in the wee hours of the next day I found my Savior. Soon afterwards I became a serious student of the Bible. My group of young friends and I started digging into the Word, charting prophecies about the second coming, trying to figure out what was coming next. Another friend and I became deeply interested in theology and we searching the Scriptures as we studied baptism, eternal security, free will—young men like to study doctrine.

In the years since I've come to faith I've seen a lot of different approaches to studying the Word. There was the traveling salesman I met who wasn't a believer but read one chapter of Proverbs every day of the month to try to be a better person. He really didn't like it when there were thirty-one days in the month because he had to read about the Proverbs 31 woman. I know of a preacher who for thirty years never preached a series from the Old Testament because he didn't know where to find Jesus except in a few isolated prophecies. I met a woman at a conference who told me she only read the book of Genesis because it contained every doctrine of the Bible. There was the young woman who showed me how she'd tabbed her Bible for character traits she wanted to instill in her children. I've met Johnny-one-notes who use the Bible to proof-text their political positions. One man told me the point of Joseph's story was that government handouts are wrong.

We can so easily miss the meaning of the story, and when we do our hearts grow cold. I didn't realize it but I was moving away from my first love in those years after I came to faith, in large part because I wasn't seeing Jesus in all the Scriptures; I wasn't seeing the storyline. Finally in my twenties I became Jonah and left the Lord behind.

By God's grace, in my thirties I came back, married, and started attending seminary. I'll never forget sitting in my first Old Testament course expecting the professor to turn to Genesis and being completely taken by surprise when he opened up to Luke 24 instead. It's the story of that first Easter morning when Jesus appeared to two very discouraged disciples and showed them how the Scriptures were all pointing to him all along. "Beginning with Moses and all the Prophets, he explained to them what was said in all the Scriptures concerning himself." Jesus not only explained this on the Road to Emmaus, he went over it again when he appeared to the eleven back in Jerusalem. He even explained it to the Pharisees weeks before he died. "You study the Scriptures diligently because you think that in them you have eternal life. These are the very Scriptures that testify about me."

That day in class it finally clicked. It's one Great Story of redemption that glows with the glory of Jesus from beginning to end. Jesus gave us the key that unlocks the beauty of the story and makes us weep from sheer joy. Once I had that key in hand the Bible started opening up and it's been opening up ever since. It just keeps getting richer and more saturated with good news. Jesus just keeps getting bigger and more glorious.

Sally Lloyd-Jones has written *The Jesus Storybook Bible* for children where every single story testifies to Jesus. She had her own Copernican revolution in how she read the Bible and developed a passion for children to hear it that way too. It's so easy to turn the focus away from Jesus, and Sally witnessed a perfect demonstration of what happens when we do. She was teaching a Sunday school class of six-year-olds, telling them the story of the ever-faithful God who rescued Daniel from the lion's den and how this same God had promised to send another Rescuer who would pull off the greatest rescue the world had ever seen. She then joyfully announced the wonderful news that the Rescuer had come and that his name is Jesus.

Sally said, "One little girl in particular was sitting so close to me she was almost in my lap. Her face was bright and eager as she listened to the story, utterly captivated. She could hardly keep on the ground and kept kneeling up to get closer to the story."[2]

But then, "At the end . . . there were no other teachers around, and I panicked and went into automatic pilot and heard myself—to my horror—asking, "And so what can we learn from Daniel about how God wants us to live?" And as I said those words it was as if I had literally laid a huge load on that little girl. Like I broke some spell. She crumpled right in front of me, physically slumping and bowing her head. I will never forget it."[3]

That's what happens when we make the Bible all about us instead of all about Jesus. We slump. It happens to children and it happens to us. God didn't give us these stories so we'd turn men into heroes and try to emulate their lives. They're meant to be pictures of the coming Redeemer. Joseph's story whispers a glorious truth about the One to come, the suffering Messiah who is going to endure rejection at the hands of his brothers for their salvation. Every story in the Bible was fore-planned by God to enrich his narrative and enlarge our understanding of Jesus. Each installment raises our hopes that this is the answer at last, and then lets us down so we'll keep waiting.

God promises Abraham a great multitude of offspring who will inherit the land and bless the nations but the whole thing seems to fizzle out. God uses Moses to accomplish a great exodus but the people break faith again and again. He promises that one of David's sons will be the heir of the nations but king follows king until things are so bad God removes the people from the land. They're carried off into exile and we weep and weep as if our hearts would break. Is the world dead yet? No it's not! With every failure of the people, God makes his promises bigger and richer until we're leaning hard on God's shoulder, wondering how he can possibly pull it off. Will anyone ever be worthy to open the scroll?

Then he amazes us with the coming of Jesus, expected and yet unexpected, awesome in how it resolves everything in one glorious finale. The impossibility of redemption becomes possible when God gives up his Son to death and then raises him to life again. The world is alive, we're alive, because the triumph of Christ has unlocked the scroll and saved the day. God has put creation back in its orbit and re-centered his world on the One who is worthy.

That's our story. It's big; it's glorious; and it has the power to engage our hearts and expand our lives.

But there's another story. Our enemy is spinning another tale, one where God is out of the picture and we're endowed with the inalienable right to live as we choose. Ultimately there are only two stories: God's story or the enemy's story, the story that brings life or the story that brings death, the truth or the lie.

Some version of the lie is coming at us all the time, in a thousand different guises, but they all have this in common—they put us at the center and say, "Once upon a time there was you and it's all about you." Open any magazine, listen to any talk show, go in to any bookstore and you'll hear that story. It can come in the form of a promise that our individual dream is meant to come true or it can be a full-blown myth, a sweeping tale of where we come from and where we're headed.

C. S. Lewis wrote an essay about how nineteenth-century literature rewrote the human story along these lines. In this rewrite, "to exist means to be moving from the status of 'almost zero' to the status of 'almost infinity.'"[4] There is no "god" to restrict our behavior or put limits on what we might become. We are the potential gods. You can look around us today and see how that megamyth not only captured the imagination of the modern world but ushered in the postmodern world we live in which simply takes it for granted.

Lewis said that for him Christianity was the funeral of this great myth. He believed it once and only with great reluctance, as he came to faith in Christ, was he forced to let it die. "It is our painful duty as Christians," he said, "to wake the world from this enchantment."[5] If you know the Narnia tales you can probably hear the voice of Puddleglum coming through in those words. In the story of Prince Rilian, Puddleglum had to awaken the prince from an evil spell by stamping his foot in the fire, thus filling the room with the smell of burnt Marshwiggle. As Christians it may be our painful duty to wake the world from its enchantment through our suffering—but it's also our painful duty to wake ourselves. We need to realize when we've started chanting the mantra. We need to shake our heads and remember that its origins go back further than the nineteenth century, back all the way to the genesis of the world, when the deceiver cast his spell on Eve by re-imagining God: "He's not the Holy Creator God who made heaven and earth as an act of creative joy and then made you in his image for a love-filled relationship with himself. No, my dear. He is a powerless, self-centered demagogue who is holding you back. Just eat this fruit and you will be god."

She fell for it, she repressed the knowledge of God, and our fallen hearts have been predisposed to fall for it ever since. It seems like a new revelation every time because it's constantly reemerging in different guises, but the gist of it never changes: God is taken out of our calculations; he is reduced, defamed, or imagined out of existence, leaving us free to pursue our own destinies as the central figure of the story.

It can happen to us as believers. We can forget the true story. We can repress the knowledge of God and start living the lie. That's when we start to live small. We need to immerse ourselves in the great story of the Bible again and again. It's the great cure for the enemy's lie because it not only tells us who Jesus is—it tells us who *we* are. We are the sons and daughters of God. God not only gave us his own Son as our ransom, he re-birthed us into his own image. The lie has a zero-sum premise—the more of him the less of you. He has to go so you can expand. The truth is—the more of him, the more of us.

John was overwhelmed by this reality: "See what great love the Father has lavished on us, that we should be called children of God! And that is what we are! . . .What we will be has not yet been made known. But we know that when Christ appears we shall be like him, for we shall see him as he is." We shall be like him. He's bringing us into his glory. The incomprehensible generosity of God pulls the fangs right out of the enemy's lie.

Ask Ridley Herschell. We read his story in a compilation of remarkable testimonies by Jewish believers, and it touched us both deeply. Ridley was raised an Orthodox Jew in Europe during the nineteenth century, but when he left home to study at the university he jettisoned his childhood beliefs in favor of the prevalent myth—the one C. S. Lewis described in his essay. For a while he enjoyed a heady sense of freedom but eventually the knowledge of God started beating in him like a telltale heart. It was so relentless it drove him back to his Orthodox practices. They didn't help. Nothing relieved his sense of alienation, which finally became so intense he prayed the first spontaneous, unscripted prayer of his life, "Oh God, I have no one to help me! Help, Oh help me!"[6] This is what happened.

He went into a shop to buy a small item—he doesn't say what it was. The shopkeeper wrapped it in a page taken from an old, repurposed book. Walking home he happened to glance at the wrapper and was struck by the words: "Blessed are the poor in spirit, for theirs is the kingdom of heaven." He had no idea where they came from, but he was intrigued. A few days later at the house of a friend he saw a New Testament lying on a table. Curious, he thumbed through until he came to Matthew 5 and his eyes fell on these words, "Blessed are the poor in spirit: for theirs is the kingdom of heaven" (v. 3). He borrowed the book and started reading a little bit every day but the name of Jesus was so shocking he keep throwing it aside. Then he would go dig it out and read some more, only to throw it away again.

Finally he resolved to read the books of Moses instead, starting with Genesis. This was safer ground. When he got to Genesis 3, the reason for his own unhappiness jumped right off the page. He saw that "The subtle enemy . . . succeeded . . . in his attempt to instill into the minds of our first parents . . . doubt of the love of God."[7] Ridley immediately recognized the roots of his own alienation. He realized that this was his very own story and that it was telling him life's crucial question. It boils down to this: "How can I be reconciled to God?"

The answer was quick to come. God promised to send a "seed" of the woman to undo the work of the serpent. But how could he do it? To Herschell the answer seemed obvious: "He must so exhibit the love of God to man as to draw forth man's love in return. . . . It must be a love that can with consistency to the perfect holiness of God be extended toward a guilty and rebellious people."[8]

But if the seed is just one more fallen person, how can he do this? He would have to be born without sin. He would have to be an intermediary with one hand on God and one hand on man. He would have to be (he shrank from the thought) the incarnation of Deity as man.

Herschell saw where this was headed and he didn't like it. Still, he kept on reading and found that Christ just kept throwing light on everything he read in the Old Testament. As he says, "Though I had thrown aside the New Testament, I could not get rid of the light I had acquired from it."[9] Theologians call this "*sensus plenior,*" which means "fuller meaning." In retrospect, now that Jesus has come, we can see the fuller meaning of every story and we have it on good authority that this is the way we're meant to read the Bible: "It is . . . clear that Jesus and the apostles regarded the whole of the Old Testament as a testimony to the Christ; it is *all* about Jesus."[10]

> *We want to believe the story of our redemption, but we look around us and it doesn't connect.*

For Ridley it was the theme of the lamb that started making sense. All through the story there's this need for an atoning sacrifice. Every time the sacrificial lamb would crop up, Herschell would remember the prayer he'd said as a child on the Day of Atonement, "Raise up for us an upright advocate; and cause the backslider to hear: 'I have found a ransom.'"

He knew the New Testament claimed that Jesus was this God-given ransom but he was afraid to believe it. He feared not only the rejection of his family but the loss of his own identity. Finally, with his back to the wall, he conceded the point—Jesus was the Messiah. Still he couldn't bring himself to accept him as the answer to his own pain until these words came into his mind, "Up until now you have asked nothing in my name."

He remembered whose words they were, that Jesus spoke them the night before he died. He also remembered the rest of what Jesus said, "Ask now and you will receive." After a great battle with bone-deep resistance he accepted the offer and asked in his name, "Lord, I believe that Jesus is the Messiah, the Redeemer, and King of Israel, who was wounded for our transgressions. For his sake have mercy on me and give me peace." Herschell says, "No sooner had I offered this prayer than . . . the peace of God . . . entered into my soul. I felt that I was redeemed from destruction, that God loved me, that Christ had died for me and washed me from all my sins in his own blood."[11]

The story led Herschell to Jesus. It set him free from his self-preoccupation by giving him a glorious new identity in Jesus. And that's what it's meant to do for us. The problem is, sometimes our lives seem to be telling another story. We want to believe the story of our redemption but we look around us and it doesn't connect. In her book *One Thousand Gifts* Ann Voskamp puts into words this disconnect that many of us feel from God's story. She was four years old when her memory was jolted awake by the sight of her little sister's crushed body cradled in her mother's rocking arms. Her parents pled with God but the answer didn't come and from that point on they closed down on God. She says that when her sister was buried, any notion of God's grace was buried with her.

Years later, after she'd become a believer, married her farmer husband, and given birth to six children, Ann still had that legacy of the fall etched in her heart. She tells about waking up in the morning and believing "the Serpent's hissing lie, the repeating refrain of his campaign through the ages: God isn't good. It's the cornerstone of his movement. That God withholds good from his children, that God does not genuinely, fully, love us."[12] She says her soul would heal once a week when she went to church but the rest of the week she lived in pain.

Many of us can relate to Ann's story. We're missing the grace of the great story because the hard things in our lives are telling us another tale. We need God to speak the truth into our hearts, to tell us plainly what his purpose for our life really is. It came through to Ann when she read 1 Corinthians 2:7: "His secret purpose framed from the very beginning [is] to bring us to our full glory" (NEB).

"He means to rename us," Ann says, "to return us to our true names, our truest selves. He means to heal our soul holes. From the very beginning, that Eden beginning, that has always been and always is to this day, His secret purpose—to return us to our full glory."[13]

Ann longed to live the fullness of this glory; she yearned to come alive to the truth of the story right here and now. She had a deep hunger for joy and she found the answer when she read how Jesus "took bread, gave thanks and broke it, and gave it to them." She realized God had placed a table of grace right at the center of our faith and that we're meant to respond to it by giving thanks. Thanksgiving is what brings us into the reality of our salvation and fills us with joy.

Paul says the people who repress the knowledge of God never give him thanks. Ingratitude is a deeply ingrained habit of our fallen hearts but we can reverse the trend. We can pour out our gratitude for the magnificent gift of his Son, for how he entered into our pain and with his death and resurrection rewrote our story. We can give him thanks for the promise that some day we'll be given the sensus plenior of our own stories, the meaning of everything we've lived through, even the pain. We can give him thanks for all the small gifts he floods into our lives every day, gifts we typically miss without giving a thought to the Giver.

A friend dared Ann to do this, to make a list of one thousand blessings. She started by writing down three: "Morning shadows across the old floor, jam piled high on the toast, cry of blue jay from high in the spruce."[14] It became a habit; this giving a name to every little gift of God, and with the habit came a deep change in her vision. She began to see him everywhere, extravagantly pouring forth his love in the details of her life. Eventually this practice of giving thanks took her full circle back to the greatest gift of all. She was driving to church for early morning nursery duty when the culminating truth of the story hit her full-force. "'He who did not spare his own Son but gave him up for us all—how will he not also, along with him, graciously give us all things?' He gave us Jesus. *Jesus! Gave Him up for us all!* If we only have one memory isn't that enough? . . . The counting of all blessings is ultimately summed up in One. And the radical wonder of it stuns me happy, hushes me still: *it's all Christ.* Every moment, every event, every happening. *It's all in Christ and in Christ we are always safe.*"[15]

Notes

1. aholyexperience.com, "The Best Read Ever," March 24, 2010.

2. desiringgod.org, "Teach Children the Bible Is Not About Them," July 12, 2012.

3. Ibid.

4. C. S. Lewis, *Christian Reflections* (Grand Rapids: Eerdmans, 1967), 86.

5. Ibid., 93.

6. Ridley Herschell, *Jewish Witnesses That Jesus Is the Christ* (London: Aylott & Jones, 8, Paternoster-Row, 1923), 6.

7. Ibid., 15.

8. Ibid., 18.

9. Ibid., 19.

10. Graeme Goldsworthy, *Gospel-Centered Hermeneutics* (Westmont, Ill.: IVP Academic, 2006), 251.

11. Herschell,, *Jewish Witnesses*, 30.

12. Ann Voskamp, *One Thousand Gifts* (Grand Rapids: Zondervan, 2010), 14.

13. Ibid., 17.

14. Ibid., 45.

15. Ibid., 155.

3

The Work of One Who Lives

When you live in a small town, the funeral home gets to be familiar territory. Even when you move away you keep coming back. We'd been there countless times for the funerals of friends and family but this time it was different. Now it was our turn to sit in the office and discuss clothes and how difficult it would be to make him look presentable after such a long time. It was our turn to receive the special hushed treatment and the generic condolences, our turn to choose between the brass and the brushed steel casket.

We didn't want it to be our turn—but it was. Our son's body would soon be arriving from California to be buried in his Oklahoma hometown and we were making plans for the funeral. The drive through town earlier in the day had flooded us with memories of snow cones and sandboxes and a little blond mite of a boy with big blue eyes playing Dukes of Hazzard in his Cozy Coupe. We'd watched Jeff struggle for most of his twenty-one years, praying for him and trying desperately to intervene, but in the end his drug addiction won the day. Still, he'd believed in Jesus, clung to him as his Savior, and in the midst of our staggering grief we had great hope that this wasn't the end—that Jesus had saved him.

The Lord had been with us through it all, making his presence known in precious and powerful ways. Even in that air-conditioned office, with the reality of Jeff's death hitting us hard amidst the pastel colors and the elevator music, we were clinging to the fact that there's more to life—and to death—than what our eyes can see. As believers we're living our part in the story in this final age between the first and second appearances of the Lord, and we need the eyes of faith to do it. Jesus was here once and his disciples got to see him with their physical eyes. He walked down dusty roads, cooked fish over charcoal fires, and slept in the back of boats. John gropes to convey the exquisite marvel of living in the same physical space with Jesus: "We've seen, we've heard, we've touched with our hands" (see 1 John 1:1). He entered our concrete world and to our great joy became bone of our bone and flesh of our flesh but then he ascended and he won't enter the range of our vision again until his return.

But he's not gone. Even though we can't see him with our physical eyes, he's still here. He's not far removed from us way up in heaven somewhere. Artists know that to make an object look far away they have to paint it small and faded. When we think of Jesus as distant from us, he can seem to get smaller and fade from our "sight." We need to remember his promise: "I will not leave you as orphans; I will come to you. Before long, the world will not see me anymore, but you will see me. Because I live, you also will live."

The story isn't just on the pages of the Bible, it's continuing right now, we're living it, and he's right here with us. We each have a personal exodus story to tell of how we hunkered down under the protection of the blood of the Lamb while judgment passed over us and landed on him. We've each one passed through the Red Sea of his death and through his resurrection entered a new life of freedom. We're in the final installment of the story, heading together toward a new heaven and the new earth, and he's with us—just like he was with the Israelites in the wilderness when he traveled with them and filled the tabernacle with his presence. Only now he's with us in our own flesh and blood. Now we each have an intimate connection with him that can never be broken.

For almost two thousand years the church has declared, "He is risen," and in response has thundered back, "He is risen indeed!" That joyous confidence comes from a profound knowledge that Jesus really is alive. He may be unseen but we can see him by faith, as paradoxical as it sounds. The world can't see him but we can—faintly at times and at other times with a palpable reality that takes our breath away.

We're called to live that faith, even when life seems to shout out a contradiction to everything we believe. Right at that point we can fight the battle. We can open the Bible and fill up on the story. We can call a believing friend and have a conversation about the Lord. We can preach the truth to our own hearts and then give thanks as if it's really true, because it is. We can ask the Spirit to help us to see the unseen things and know that he will because that's what he does—he renews us day by day. "We do not lose heart. Though outwardly we are wasting away, yet inwardly we are being renewed day by day. For our light and momentary troubles are achieving for us an eternal glory that far outweighs them all. So we fix our eyes not on what is seen, but on what is unseen, since what is seen is temporary, but what is unseen is eternal."

At the graveside, the reality of the resurrection rang out with power into the shimmering August heat.

We couldn't see the Lord Jesus with our physical eyes that sorrowful week we buried our son but he was there, preaching good news to our broken hearts. We needed help; we needed reinforcements and they came in the form of believing friends, sent by the Lord. First came

Cyndi and Lanning, driving across those great empty spaces between Colorado and Oklahoma, drawn as they told us later by a loving urgency just to be there with us. We arranged to meet at Braum's, a fluorescent-lit ice-cream place with big booths where we could visit in private. After we talked awhile we told them we'd been discussing Romans 1:11–12 on the drive to Braum's. Paul was telling the Christians in Rome he couldn't wait to see them because he knew they would be mutually encouraged by each other's faith. Cyndi and Lanning had done that for us. We knew how much we needed them to build up our faith and we thanked them for doing it. Cyndi's jaw dropped and she leaned forward and said, "We talked about that exact verse all the way here. It was our theme verse—the reason we came. We didn't know what we could do, but we thought maybe just being with you would encourage your faith."

Those hard days of grief taught us like never before just how much we need other believers in order to live this life of faith we're called to live. Wave after wave of believing friends arrived on the scene. They brought their faith in Jesus, that he had accomplished a great redemption, and it filled us with hope. They brought their certainty that Jesus trumps every loss and we experienced the truth of it.

Then again at the graveside, when our son's precious body was about to disappear into the wounded ground, our preacher son-in-law began to read from 1 Corinthians 15 and the reality of the resurrection cut right through the whir of the cicadas and the rustle of the scrub oaks and rang out with power into the shimmering August heat:

Listen, I tell you a mystery: We will not all sleep, but we will all be changed—in a flash, in the twinkling of an eye, at the last trumpet. For the trumpet will sound, the dead will be raised imperishable, and we will be changed . . . Then the saying that is written will come true: "Death has been swallowed up in victory."

The Lord preached his victory into our hearts as those words were read and it wasn't just a dormant hope, lying dead in the ground, waiting for the last trump to sound. It was a rising joy and it triumphed in the face of our pain. The crucified, resurrected Jesus filled us with the substance of his victory on the cross and it was like Easter morning all over again. It really was. Our grief was still there but it was swallowed up in a great tearful joy. It was more than a promise for the future; it was power of the resurrection breaking right into a dog day of an Oklahoma summer and giving us life.

After the funeral, our youngest son, Peter, went home with our daughter, Kate, and her family for a visit before he headed back to California. They all piled into the minivan and made the long trip from Oklahoma to eastern Washington with Peter and his three-year-old niece playing many games of I Spy along the way. It started less than an hour into the trip:

"Uncle Peter, I spy something gray."

"Hmmm, okay, Charlotte, is it my T-shirt?"

"No."

"Is it your carseat?"

"No."

"Is it the dashboard?"

"What's a dashboard?"

The game went on and on until Peter finally surrendered:

"Okay, Charlotte, I give up. What is it?"

"It's my imaginary elephant!" Charlotte announced in triumph.

"No, Charlotte," Peter groaned, "it has to be something real!"

It has to be something real—and it is. As believers in Jesus we're spying the rock-solid reality of life. One fine day he'll burst into the physical realm and every eye on earth will see him. Until then we live by faith. We keep fixing our eyes on the unseen things and learning to live every day like it's Easter.

Mary Magdalene was heartbroken when she saw the empty tomb on that first Easter morning. She assumed Jesus' body had been stolen and that she'd lost even the bittersweet consolation of preparing it for burial. Every biography in the Bible ends in the same defeating way and Mary thought it was happening all over again, that never-ending victory of the grave. But then she heard him say her name and her world changed. The entire universe changed when God brought Jesus back to life. That single epic act of power is reverberating into the world with great good news. Jesus truly is the Son of God—the resurrection proclaims it loud and clear. Jesus truly is the uncontested victor in the battle he waged on the cross—the resurrection sings it like a hallelujah chorus.

The old sin-stained, death-defeated world was left behind when Jesus was raised and a brand-new, God-glorious creation came into existence—and we're part of it, right now, even in the midst of our brokenness and suffering. Jesus is here, pouring the resurrection into our hearts. He's here in his church giving her strength—standing amongst the lampstands like he was when John saw him nearly two thousand years ago. He's here in the world invading the enemy's territory and spreading his blood-bought kingdom to the far reaches of the earth. The story is still unfolding and we can see the evidence all around us if we know where to look.

Last year I flew to Malawi and then drove many bumpy hours into the bush to take a look at the village of Dzuwa. Lying under the mosquito netting in my cot that first night I could hear the high-pitched hum of a malaria-bearing mosquito hovering relentlessly only inches away from my face with just that very thin netting separating me from her bloodsucking intentions. It reminded me of the vulnerability of those village people who not long ago had been living hand to mouth in a fear-dominated culture.

A few years back our friend Fletcher Matandika was sent to this village by his pastor father to preach the gospel. It was known as a dark place where witchcraft was rampant. Two teachers had mysteriously died and the fear of the witch doctor's curse had sent most of the other teachers packing. Only two bravely stayed behind to try to cope with 540 students. When Fletcher first walked into the village he says he looked around and felt both a great peace and a great passion to see the transforming power of Christ at work. The verse on his heart was Isaiah 9:2, "The people walking in darkness have seen a great light; on those living in the land of deep darkness a light has dawned." He told his father he wanted to go back and spend a week with the people of Dzuwa, although they both knew there was a great danger he literally might not come back alive.

When he arrived back in the village he was given an empty house to stay in, a place widely considered to be invaded by witchcraft. Dark and terrifying things happened to people who spent the night in that house but Fletcher slept like a baby—until the village chief came knocking at the door at five the next morning. He'd been worried all night and was amazed and impressed to find Fletcher perfectly unharmed.

A few days later Fletcher told him he believed God had given him a dream of turning Dzuwa into a testimony to the power of Christ. He talked about microfinance, a medical facility, clean water, and irrigation—all the possibilities of transformation that could come to Dzuwa in the name of Jesus. The chief looked at him and said, "God made the world and if he wants to do something here who am I to stop him?"

Fletcher told this story on the *HAVEN Today* program five years ago, and now I was here, seeing the transformation firsthand. Every piece of Fletcher's dream had become a reality—Christians had dug wells for fresh water, new teachers had arrived, a medical clinic had been built and was saving lives, new micro-industries had sprung up, irrigation was allowing them to grow more than one crop a year. But what struck me more than anything was the dignity and freedom of the people. It reminded me of an article I read in the London *Times*. After a forty-five-year absence the journalist had returned to his home country of Malawi and was writing about what he saw, "In Africa Christianity changes people's hearts. It brings a spiritual transformation. The rebirth is real. The change is good."[1]

What's especially interesting about this testimony is that the journalist who wrote it was an atheist. He said, "The Christians were always different. Far from having cowed or confined its converts, their faith appeared to have liberated and relaxed them."[2]

> *It's heartbreaking to feast on the bread of life while your own child is sitting next to you refusing to eat.*

That's exactly what I saw in Dzuwa—the people were liberated and relaxed in Christ and their physical conditions had vastly improved. Granted, it wasn't California. I was cowering under my mosquito netting to avoid more than malaria. My African brothers had warned me to take a flashlight to the privy because they'd killed a black mamba the week before. I'd never heard of a black mamba but it didn't sound good. Later I learned it's one of the deadliest snakes on the planet and that it doesn't slither off into the bush at the sound of human footsteps either, it comes after you. I was awake most of the night listening to the buzzing of the mosquito; feeling the growing pressure on my bladder; and rejoicing in the awesome things I'd seen in Dzuwa that day. But I was also rejoicing in something else—something even closer to my heart.

That evening the African missionaries and an American couple I knew, a young Army chaplain and his wife, had all gathered for a Malawian meal of nsima. Lindsey was suffering greatly after five days without a shower or a shampoo, but her husband Stephen was irrepressible. He exuberantly told everyone at the table about a wonderful work of the Lord he had witnessed a few years ago. He had supported himself through seminary as a night watchman at our church in California and while he was there he organized a weekly prayer meeting. He told how he and about ten other people had prayed for our son, Peter, and about the miracle that happened just one week later.

Peter had gone from being an apparently committed Christian to an agnostic practically overnight in his senior year of high school. Janet and I both vividly remember the first Sunday morning he passed the communion basket without taking a piece for himself. It's heartbreaking to feast on the bread of life while your own child is sitting next to you refusing to eat. About a year after Jeff's death, after a year studying at a local university, Peter left to live with friends in Portland, Oregon. Finally, to avoid living on the streets, he moved in with Kate and her family. Within a few months he'd made contact with a young woman on the Internet and they had moved in together in her uncle's home.

And then the prayer meeting happened. I was out of town but Janet went armed with a very specific prayer request. She'd been reading Matthew 3 where Jesus went to be baptized in the Jordan. When he came out of the water the Holy Spirit descended on him like a dove and the Father said, "This is my beloved Son in whom I am well-pleased." When dear Janice Baldwin asked how they could pray for Peter, Janet told them, "Pray that he would be united to Jesus by faith, that the Spirit would descend on him like a dove and that the Father would say, 'This is my beloved son in whom I am well pleased.'" She wanted the full-orbed trinity of blessings right here in the land of the living. Janice prayed and the meeting dismissed.

The next day Janet was praying for Peter again in the kitchen and the way she tells it, a word from the Lord just drenched her with joy and said, "The old has gone, the new has come." A couple of days later

I got a call from the girlfriend's uncle. He had just discovered that both his niece and our Peter were using drugs and wanted to know what to do. I'd had a lot more experience with drug addiction than I wanted but I knew what to tell him to do, at least in the short run. I said, "Tell them they're going to be in one of two places by the end of the day—either out on the street or in a detox facility—better yet, separate detox facilities."

Janet and I immediately packed our bags and started driving up the West Coast. I was worried we might lose another son but pleading with God to come through, and I felt compelled that we needed to be there. Janet was completely relaxed. She kept telling me, "The old has gone, the new has come."

Kate heard the news and started driving with her family over the Cascades from eastern Washington. She'd made up her mind that Peter was going to accept Jesus as his Savior whether he liked it or not. She'd talked to him about this more than once when he lived with them and had recently written him a long, impassioned letter. Now she was determined to employ whatever big-sister bossiness she had at her disposal to make it happen. As she puts it, "I wasn't going to lose another brother." She reached Peter a day before we did and found him deeply heartbroken that he'd allowed this to happen. They talked awhile and then Kate made her fighting pitch. "Peter, Jesus is the only answer. You have to accept him as your Savior right now." Peter looked at her and said, "I did, Katie, last night. I asked him to give me a new life."

Peter spent a year in Teen Challenge and now seven years later he's married to a young woman he met at Moody Bible Institute, the lovable, lovely Katrina, and finishing a Master of Divinity before they head off to South America to serve as missionaries. But what I was remembering under the mosquito netting was the day he left detox. It was late in the afternoon when we picked him up and the sun was setting gold and glorious. We checked into a hotel, Peter had a shower, and then we told him to order anything he wanted off the menu. "Go ahead and get the most expensive steak, the finest fatted calf they have to offer." The next morning before going to church we asked Peter if he wanted to read Isaiah with us. Janet and I had been reading a chapter a day and we had arrived at chapter 9. Peter said, "Sure." He took the Bible and read, "The people walking in darkness have seen a great light; on those living in the land of deep darkness a light has dawned." All three of us started crying for joy.

Our world thinks it's dealt with Christianity, deconstructed it out of existence, dusted off its hands and moved on.

Jesus is alive and powerfully at work in his world, and we can see it in the transformed lives of his people. Athanasius (293–373) was a church father who wrote a defense of the reality of the resurrection and his primary argument was the otherwise inexplicable transformation of so many pagans:

> Look at the facts of the case. The Savior is working mightily among men, every day. He is invisibly persuading numbers of people all over the world to accept his faith and be obedient to his teaching. Can anyone in the face of this still doubt that he has risen and lives . . . ? Does a dead man prick the consciences of men so they throw all the traditions of their fathers to the winds and bow down before the teaching of Christ? If he is no longer active in the world . . . how is it that he makes the adulterer [cease] from his adultery, the murderer from murdering . . . ? This is the work of one who lives, not of the dead; and more than that, it is the work of God.[3]

It's glorious to see a young man who was raised in the faith being reclaimed by the Hound of Heaven—especially when it's your own dear son. It's amazing to look back and see paganism falling to the power of the risen Christ all those centuries ago—and to see it falling today in places like Africa.

But what about here, in this post-Christian Western world? It's one thing for the power of the gospel to hit the streets for the first time; but now it's being relegated to the category of old bad news. Our world thinks it's dealt with Christianity, deconstructed it out of existence, dusted off its hands and moved on. Marva Dawn says our Western world has become a carnival filled with "myriads of consumerist opportunities and entertaining sideshows—including those of various spiritualities."[4]

Is Jesus able to rescue people out of this enticing carnival of choices? Rosaria Butterfield is proof that he can. She writes,

> When I was twenty-eight years old, I boldly declared myself a lesbian. I was at the finish of a PhD in English Literature and Cultural Studies. I was a teaching associate in one of the first and strongest Women's Studies Departments in the nation. I was being recruited by universities to take on faculty and administrative roles in advancing radical leftist ideologies. . . . At the age of thirty-six, I was one of the few tenured women at a large research university. . . . That same year, Christ claimed me for himself and the life that I had known and loved came to a humiliating end.[5]

How did he do it, how did Christ break down those barriers and bring Rosaria to a faith so deep she speaks with hushed reverence about his redeeming blood and finds herself "at the limits of language" when she tries to describe her life in Christ? Everything was stacked against it. Not only was her postmodern worldview a seemingly insurmountable barrier, there were her encounters with the church. She was constantly getting flak from the conservative Christian community, and it wasn't pretty. The probabilities of her ever embracing the Christian faith were seemingly nil. Nil, that is, unless you factor in the resurrected Jesus.

Jesus says Satan is like a strong man fully armed who's guarding his house. His possessions are safe unless someone stronger attacks him and overpowers him, takes away his armor and divides the spoil. Satan has carried us all away as spoil but Jesus is the stronger man. Jesus broke the enemy's power on the cross and now he's systematically robbing his house and claiming his own for himself. It's awesome to see how he claimed Rosaria.

First she met a pastor who broke through her strongly reinforced expectations of how Christians treat people like herself. He and his wife showed her kindness and respect. They spent quality time with her until eventually she considered them friends. Ken encouraged her to explore the kinds of questions she admired as an academic: "How did you arrive at your interpretations? How do you know you're right?" She realized her postmodern views were based on unexamined presuppositions but her commitment to openness made her willing to reconsider them. Ken's view of the Bible clearly violated a fundamental premise she had previously accepted without question: There are no truths, only truth claims. Truth claims can't claim you. But the truth is another matter. Could there be such a thing as truth?

Rosaria felt she had to at least be open to the possibility. She started going to church to hear Ken's sermons. She studied the Bible; she even studied the original languages to try to get at the heart of it all. In the process she became convinced that it was true. It didn't just claim to be true; it authenticated itself to her heart. It communicated its truth just the way John Calvin says it does: "Scripture exhibits . . . its own truth as sweet and bitter things do . . . [by] their taste" (John

Calvin, *Institutes*).[6] Rosaria tasted truth like honey. She says it was beautiful to realize there was a "knowable, dependable, sturdy, and comprehensive idea of truth and a man-god who so loved his people that he endured the wrath of God the Father for the sins that I had committed and those I would go on to commit."[7]

The battle was intense but in the end this is what happened, in her own words: "I prayed and asked God if the gospel message was for someone like me. . . . I viscerally felt the living presence of God as I prayed. Jesus seemed present and alive. I knew that I was not alone in my room. I prayed that if Jesus was truly a real and risen God, that he would change my heart. . . . I asked him to take it all: my sexuality, my profession, my community, my tastes, my books, and my tomorrows."[8]

God hadn't even been a thought in Rosaria's mind and yet somehow, in that mysterious way he has, the Spirit empowered the Word and her perception of reality began to change. The Lord began to take on weight and substance, until finally his Word became the one overriding factor in her life. It was bigger than the right she felt to her own opinions, bigger than the deep bond she had with her community, bigger than her hard-won academic standing—bigger even than the fundamental identity she had crafted for herself.

Jesus said those "who love the truth recognize that what I say is true." Those who want the truth regardless of the cost will be able to hear it. And it always has a cost. At the very least we're required to surrender our self-determination but the cost is often higher—sometimes even death.

For Rosaria the losses were extreme and they could easily have won the day but in the end the balance tipped in favor of the Word of God. She says at first it just barely tipped. "The word of God had gotten to be bigger inside of me than I was, bigger by about the size of a hair."[9] Still, it's impressive to see how that little extra weight supplied the courage she needed to opt for the Lord and walk away from her former life. It was an unraveling of her very self but she did it because

God's Word had become the one non-negotiable thing.

Then, as she puts it, the "train wreck" hit. Her life was derailed, crumpled, destroyed, and she had to pick her painful way through the wreckage. She's now a living, breathing testimony to the fact that Jesus is alive and potently active in his world. As Athanasius put it, "This is the work of one who lives, not of the dead; and more than that, it is the work of God." Jesus is still writing his story.

Notes

1. Matthew Parris, *As An Atheist I Believe Africa Needs God* (The London *Times*: December 27, 2008).

2. Ibid.

3. Athanasius, *On the Incarnation* (Crestwood, NY: St Vladimir's Seminary Press, 1996), 61.

4. Marva Dawn, *A Royal Waste of Time* (Grand Rapids: Eerdmans, 1999), 51.

5. Rosaria Butterfield, *The Secret Thoughts of an Unlikely Convert* (Pittsburgh: Crown and Covenant, 2012), x.

6. John Calvin, *The Institutes of Christian Religion I* (Louisville: Westminster Press, 1960), 76.

7. Butterfield, *Secret Thoughts*, 13.

8. Ibid., 21.

9. Ibid., 49.

Part 2

BEING THE GUEST

Relaxing in Him

It was a privilege to meet the man. His book had opened our eyes to the majesty of God years ago. Now, thirty-five years later, Charles was sitting in Dr. Packer's book-lined office at Regent College with a microphone in hand, asking him questions and recording his quiet answers, and I (Janet) was getting to listen. At the end of their time together Charles posed a final question, "Dr. Packer, would you share with our Haven listeners what you've learned about Jesus since you wrote *Knowing God*?" He looked up at the ceiling, thought for a moment, and then said: "I have learned that Jesus is not Jeeves." He paused and than added, "Jesus is central, you see."

He went on to explain that Jeeves is a valet in a series of books by the late British humorist P. G. Wodehouse. Jeeves's entire life is devoted to waiting hand and foot on the rich and idle Bertie Wooster. Bertie is constantly getting himself into inane situations and Jeeves is constantly getting him out of them. At the age of eighty-something Packer felt he'd really grasped the fact that Jesus is not playing this role in our lives. We are not at the center of things with Jesus standing patiently by ready to step in whenever we might need his assistance, and then discreetly withdrawing until we need him again.

I (Janet) must confess that I was very slow to learn this. In the fifties everyone went to church—at least in our suburban neighborhood they did. There was a car pulling out of every driveway on Sunday morning, with a mother and a father sitting in the front seat and some dressed-up kids in the back seat and everybody heading off to church without any seat belts. By God's grace, Jesus introduced himself to me in my second grade Sunday school class. I remember thinking, "Jesus is the most wonderful person in the entire world." Somehow I came to know that he wasn't just "back then," but right now. I could talk to him anytime, anywhere.

I had a lot of fears as a child. Everyone seemed to know what they were doing except for me. I felt like there had been some very important meeting about life and I had missed it. But Jesus helped. I'd talk to him in bed at night and everything would be okay. But then I'd get up in the morning and be the only one in second grade who couldn't break through the Red Rover line.

As one year followed another, life felt more and more like the story of *Scuffy the Tugboat* I had read as a young child. Scuffy decided it was boring to just be a child's toy floating in the bathtub, so he headed out into the wide, wide world. At first it was pleasant floating down a little brook; but then the brook joined a river and everything started to get bigger and scarier until he was finally forced out into the harbor with all the giant steamships. Growing up felt that way to me, and I had no idea how Jesus fit into it all. As I tried to maneuver my way through life and survive in the harbor I ended up leaving the Lord behind. Eventually he wasn't even my little glow light anymore; he was just a distant memory of a more innocent time.

When I went off to college the world was undergoing a major cultural upheaval and I was swept along in the current. A new moral consensus was emerging and not only did it mold my behavior, it began to shape my idea of Jesus. He reemerged in my life as a sort of hippie Jeeves, an "I'm OK, You're OK" therapist, a gentle live-and-let-live affirmer who never judged anyone, never demanded anything, and was always there when I needed help.

Then came the night of the great intersection between the life I was living and the Lord Jesus Christ. I'd been to a party and it was late when I crawled into bed, but I was too anxious to sleep. I turned on the light and opened my Phillips New Testament, looking for some reassuring words from the Lord. One of my favorite stories was in John 8 where the Pharisees caught a woman in the act of adultery. They thought Jesus was soft on the law so they brought her to him as a test. "According to the Law, Moses commanded us to stone such women to death. Now, what do you say about it?"

> *I felt like there had been some very important meeting about life and I had missed it.*

This was a tricky situation, but Jesus handled it with his usual brilliance: "Let the one among you who has never sinned throw the first stone." Of course they all slunk away. I'd read this story many times and always given it my own self-serving spin. Jesus didn't care about the law; he just didn't want the woman to feel condemned. What really bothered him were those judgmental Pharisees. That's how I'd always read it—but this time the part at the end got to me. Jesus said to the woman, "Go away now and do not sin again" and that word *sin* began to take on weight in my heart. It occurred to me that maybe Jesus had been saying, "sin no more" to me for a long time and I hadn't been listening.

Slowly it began to dawn on me that Jesus is very holy and very serious about his Word. How had I dared to treat him in such a casual way, like he and I were in a little club of mutual understanding? How could I have been so totally tuned in to other voices, including my own fears and desires, and never tuned in to him?

Worst of all was the fear that I'd lost what I now realized was the one thing of real value in my life—Jesus himself. I cried out, "Lord, please don't shut the door on me." I slept a few hours and when I woke the next morning it hit me all over again. "Lord, I am so, so sorry. Please forgive me. Please tell me the door isn't shut." In my new humbled condition I knew I didn't deserve for this to be true. It seemed right that he would exclude me from his holy presence but I asked and then I opened the New Testament.

It fell open to Luke 15 where the Pharisees were complaining, "This man welcomes sinners and even eats his meals with them" (PHILLIPS). In the past those words would have instantly reassured me, "Of course, Jesus accepts sinners—he doesn't judge people." But now I read them and thought, "How can this be true? How can the holy Lord of glory, whose very presence excludes me because of my sin, how can he be friends with someone like me?" How do I reconcile the holy Jesus I experienced last night with this Jesus who is willing to be an intimate friend of sinners? I asked him, "Lord, how can this be?"

> *I wanted him big. I wanted him to stake his claim on me and deliver me out of the anxiety of serving other gods.*

Immediately two words came into my heart—"the cross." They came straight from Jesus and filled me with an overwhelming sense of his love. The Lord of glory suffered this terrible violence to his body so the door could be torn down and he and I could have a relationship. He took my presumptuous, appalling sin into himself, and died in my place so we could be friends. The holy Jesus did this for love of me. If he'd been there I would have washed his feet with my tears but of course he *was* there and he made me know it. I felt his presence. The door was open.

I had learned the fear of the Lord. This Jesus is not to be trifled with. But I'd also found a refuge. After that night a huge amount of anxiety drained out of my heart. I had to make major changes, end a significant relationship, but there was a new fiber in my soul because I had Jesus and nothing else mattered. It was enough to just have him, to be filled with the sweetness of knowing him. And to know he wanted all of me—that was sweetness too. Our pastor, Ted Hamilton, recently said in a sermon that Jesus refuses to be marginalized. I knew it and I was glad. I wanted him big. I wanted him to stake his claim on me and deliver me out of the anxiety of serving other gods.

What I didn't know yet, and what I still need to grasp all these many years later, is how totally complete my salvation is. The refuge is an infinite place and I never have to leave it. I start thinking I have to fill in some of the gaps or qualify somehow for his grace and then the anxiety starts seeping back in. I need to see that Jesus has done it all and that I can just relax in him. Sometimes we miss Jesus because we miss the completeness of what we have in him.

"You call me 'Teacher' and 'Lord,'" Jesus told his disciples in the upper room, "and rightly so, for that is what I am." He was affirming his cosmic centrality, his right to the throne, his prerogative to command and to be obeyed. He is not Jeeves. But the astounding thing I need to see again and again is that when he said those words he had just done something for his disciples that only the lowest of servants ever did. It was a task so demeaning that Jewish servants were never asked to perform it—only Gentiles. John tells it very intentionally, as if every detail was a slow motion miracle: Jesus had his disciples sit down, he took off his outer clothes, he wrapped a towel around his waist, he poured water into a basin, he knelt down before them, and he began to wash their feet.

Jesus is our Teacher and Lord, and yet here he is—acting as our servant. All through the Scriptures from the opening scene on the stage of creation it seems to be other way around. The Creator speaks and the physical world obeys by coming into existence. The man and woman are lovingly fashioned in his image to be in relationship with him, but it's a relationship where the Creator has the prerogative to command and they have a fundamental responsibility to obey. Jesus is this Creator and he's also the Son of David the Messiah, and as Psalm 72:11 says, "May all kings bow down to him and all nations serve him."

Yet here he is, this Messiah, this Son of God, not being served but serving us. This is the breathtaking surprise of the story. God came to minister to us, to provide for us, to lift the burden off of us. He came to do everything for us—everything we can't do for ourselves. He came to *be* everything for us—everything we can't be ourselves. This is where the story was heading all along—God will do it all. God will become our salvation.

When Herschell Ridley came to faith he says he experienced what Jesus was talking about in that late night conversation with Nicodemus. Nicodemus was completely befuddled by Jesus' statement that, "You must be born again." Herschell said he would have given the exact same answer that Nicodemus gave, "How can a man do this?" But Jesus was incredulous that a teacher in Israel could have failed to grasp the fundamental moral of the story: man can't, but God can. Somehow Israel's teachers had missed the two major themes that run straight through their story: What is impossible with man—is possible with God. As the story unfolds, Israel proves to be just as fundamentally predisposed to the lie as the rest of humanity but God meets every instance of man's failure with a promise of what he is going to do: his people need the ultimate lamb, "The Lamb of God, who takes away the sin of the world," and he's going to provide it; people need to be re-created by God's Spirit because they can't rebirth themselves, and he's going to do it. And he does. God gives his own Son to be our ransom. God rebirths us in his image as his sons and daughters by uniting us with his Son. Jesus has to endure our death so we can be raised to life in him.

God has done it all for us in Jesus. One theologian says that when a person comes to faith he "swings himself, in the totality of his being, quite off from the center of self . . . over upon Christ, now revealed to his view, as another center altogether."[1] That's what we can do. We can see that he's done it all, that he's become everything we need, and we can swing the totality of our being off ourselves and onto him.

Jesus was born a man so he could take on our obligations and fulfill them on our behalf. He walked down to the Jordan River and insisted that John baptize him along with everyone else, not because he needed to repent for his sins, but because he was stepping into our shoes. He was baptized for us and then immediately was led by the Spirit into the wilderness to be tempted for us. For forty desperately thirsty days he fought the battle we keep losing. We can read the Gospels and just sit back and watch him do it—day after day, night after night, giving himself for us, living our lives for us, obeying the Father in our stead.

Then we come to the upper room and Jesus takes off his outer clothes, wraps a towel around his waist and acts out this startling picture of what he's going to do on the cross. He's going to strip himself and become sin for us. He's going to absorb our darkness and disobedience and bear it away as far as the east is from the west. And that's what he does. He takes us beyond the need to measure up to the law, beyond judgment, out of that place where the verdict is still pending. Three days later he emerges into life and brings us with him. Everything we need—all our righteousness, all our forgiveness, all our life, all our identity, it's all in him, soup to nuts, with nothing left for us to do except receive it by faith.

Jesus is not Jeeves. To treat the glorious Son of God as our personal valet is nothing but sheer presumption but once the presumption is purged away, we can be bold believers. We can wholeheartedly believe in the fullness and finality of what Jesus has done. He wants us to do this—to live with a radical faith in his radical grace.

M y good friend Linda loves to tell stories on herself, and one of them perfectly captures the way I end up living my life when I'm not seeing the bigness of what Jesus has done. She and her husband Ted (our pastor) were in the process of moving. Ted had been a high-powered tax attorney in a Newport Beach firm but all the while he'd been chalking up billable hours he'd been quietly dreaming of preaching the gospel. Finally the Lord said, "Go." He quit the firm, went to seminary, and now they were taking a full-time pastoring position in another city. When Linda asked him what to do with all his old law books, Ted said, "Toss them." So she did. She carried them all outside, load after load, and completely filled the Dumpster with heavy legal tomes from their former life. Then she tipped it back to roll it to the street and it kept on coming, slowly falling over as she tried to get under it to push it back up. The Dumpster won and Linda was left lying on the ground, trapped underneath. It wouldn't budge no matter how hard she pushed. She heard some men working in the yard next door and started yelling for help but there was no response. Finally she realized they were speaking Spanish and somehow she dredged the word *ayudar* out of her memory. She yelled it, "*Ayudar!*" and immediately the talking stopped. She yelled it again and soon there were two very kind men lifting the Dumpster off and setting her free.

That's me. That's how I feel so often—trapped under the weight of the law—pressured by all the obligations and requirements I think I need to fulfill. I forget that Jesus has lifted that burden right off of me. Linda says it's her too, being a pastor's wife, feeling like she's living in the spotlight. The church is very gracious, she doesn't feel judged, but she judges herself. I do the same thing. We need to know where we are in the story. We need to see that Jesus has taken that legal struggle and made it a thing of the past. That was our former life; it's not the life we have in Christ.

Our friend Milton Vincent tells in his book *Gospel Primer* how much he needed to see this. He was exhausting himself trying to get into the good graces of God but he was never quite sure if he'd done it or not. Martin Luther called it the monster of uncertainty, this sense that it's up to us to get it right, that we're always on trial with the verdict still pending. That's pretty much how Milton was living his life as a pastor until one day driving home he reached the end of his rope. He was going through his usual routine, examining his own performance, sifting through his thoughts, asking the Lord, "Have I thought any thoughts that have offended you, God? Do I need to make anything right in order to restore our relationship?"[2]

Midstream into this monologue the sheer exhaustion of spending a lifetime trying to keep himself in the good favor of God took its toll. By the time he got home he was on the verge of chucking his faith. His wife and kids were away for the afternoon so he had some time alone. He picked up his Bible and started reading Romans as he paced the living room floor. He wasn't getting any help until he got to chapter five and read these words: "Therefore, since we have been justified through faith, we have peace with God through our Lord Jesus Christ, through whom we have gained access by faith into this grace in which we now stand."

It dawned on Milton that Paul's experience of the Christian life was very different from his own: He was worried about God's anger; Paul was at peace with God. He was trying to get in God's good graces; Paul knew where he stood. He was struggling to justify himself; Paul was resting in a justification he already had.

The fundamental difference was this—Milton was looking to himself but Paul was looking to Jesus. Paul understood that a cosmic judicial act had taken place when Jesus died and rose again from the dead, and that through his actions the monster of uncertainty had been put to death forever. He had peace with God, he stood in grace, because it wasn't about him—it was all about Jesus.

When God raised Jesus from the dead, he was striking the gavel and saying, "This is my beloved Son in whom I am well pleased." In a court of law the gavel rings out a message—the trial is over, the judge has ruled, the verdict is rendered. The resurrection of Jesus was just this kind of judicial act. By raising him back to life God declared that Jesus had met every requirement of his law, that he had loved God and his neighbor with every fiber of his being, that he had resisted the temptations of the evil one with absolute resolve, that he had rendered his Father a perfect obedience. That mighty act of resurrection filled the universe with the ringing declaration that Jesus is righteous—AND—that everyone who puts his faith in Jesus is righteous in him. "He was . . . raised to life for our justification," says Paul. The gavel rang out for us.

I need to remember that I can live in that bright and joyous place of my Father's everlasting favor.

We need to know this down to the depths of our soul. We need to know that the monster of uncertainty has been put to death; that we aren't outside the door wondering where we stand with God. Jesus has not only paid the price for our sins, he's earned the final, positive judgment on our behalf. We are in him and we have been declared righteous in him.

The verdict has been rendered and with that verdict comes the open door and the robe and ring and the fatted calf. That's what the prodigal found when he got home, a door flung open and his father's arms around his neck. Before he knew what was happening the servants were bringing him a robe to wear, slippers for his feet, a ring to put on his finger and his father was ordering up a lavish feast in his honor.

But some of us (like me, Janet) have trouble believing this. We can't sit easy at the table because there's this older brother standing outside bristling with disapproval and we suspect he has the law on his side. He's saying we really don't deserve to be there and we know he's right. We can't relax in the Father's house because we think we don't have a legal leg to stand on. But we do. We have Jesus' legs to stand on.

I need to remind myself of this every day because I wake up feeling like I'm in exile most mornings. I need to remember that the demands of God's law have all been met and God himself has declared me righteous in Christ. I need to remember that I can live in that bright and joyous place of my Father's everlasting favor. I need to breathe in the deep rest of being in Christ. Otherwise I end up constantly trying to justify my own existence.

The movie director Sydney Pollack said that he could never stop making movies even though the process made him frustrated and insecure because, "Every time I finish a picture, I feel like I've done what I'm supposed to do in the sense that I've earned my stay for another year or so."[3] He was on trial; he felt he had to justify his place on the planet. In his book The Freedom of Self-Forgetfulness Tim Keller quotes Madonna in an interview with Vogue where she admits to always struggling for a verdict. "Even though I have become somebody, I still have to prove that I am somebody. My struggle has never ended and I guess it never will."[4]

Apart from Jesus, the struggle never ends. We never feel like we have a right to sit at the table. We're always trying to earn it. It's a universal issue—even for atheists. We saw a live, unscripted demonstration of this at a talk we attended in Vancouver, BC. The topic was, "Does Christianity Poison Everything?" It was based on a

Christopher Hitchens book with a similar title where he tries to make the case that it does indeed poison everything. The speaker began by conceding a point to Hitchens—it's true that a great deal of wrong has been done in the name of Christ. He didn't mince words about this; in fact he spent a long time describing those wrongs, complete with visual images displayed on a screen. Then he put up a slide of a painting that showed Jesus hanging on the cross. He talked about the things Jesus taught and the life he lived and how it culminated in his death. His point was that people who do wrong in Jesus' name aren't living the way Jesus taught them to live. Christianity doesn't do harm; it's people who do harm in the name of Christianity. Then he put three more images up on the screen: Hitler, Stalin, and Pol Pot. He enumerated the atrocities they had committed in the name of other ideologies—vastly more than were ever committed in the name of Christianity. His final point was that sin is the problem for all of us and Jesus is the only answer we've got.

When it was time for questions, a woman bounded to the microphone and began unleashing a tirade of self-justification. As an atheist she was insulted by the implication that she was in the same category with those three heinous characters. She went on to tick off all the good things she had done in her life and all the wrong she had suffered at the hands of religious people. Finally the moderator had to ask for the microphone back.

Justification is a universal issue. We're all living in the courtroom, and when the finger seems to point in our direction we defend ourselves as if our life depended on it—because at some level we know it does. Paul says that God has written his law on our hearts and that our conscience anticipates the coming judgment by sometimes accusing us and sometimes even approving us. The "monster of uncertainty" never goes away because the verdict changes from day to day. If we do everything right, we'll be blessed; if we do it wrong, the blessing will be withheld. Even Christians tend to operate with this cause and effect mentality. It's just natural for humans to think in terms of karma.

Our Scottish friend Matthew was ringing up purchases for a woman at the grocery store one day. The store had a contest going and as the woman stuffed her entry into the box she said, "Wish me luck."

"I don't believe in luck," Matthew said.

She was surprised. "You don't? What about karma? Do you believe in karma?"

"Even less," he said.

"Well what do you believe in?"

She honestly wanted to know how he thought the world was wired, how the winner gets determined. Matthew kept checking her groceries as he answered her in his deepest Scottish brogue: "I believe in the sovereign grace of God."

God is the judge, he decides who wins the prize, and his judgment isn't random, it's perfectly just. God sent his Son to the cross to win the prize for us. And Jesus went willingly. He is the true older brother, the one who loves us. His heart is in perfect sync with his Father's heart. Unlike the older brother in the story of the prodigal son, Jesus doesn't point his finger and make a case for sending us away. He defends us with his own righteousness. He qualifies us to sit at the table. We live under the blessing of God all the time because of his performance, not our own.

Paul is practically speechless with amazement at what good news this is, "What can we say? If God is for us, who can be against us? Who can bring any charges against us? Who can accuse us?" (see Rom. 8:31–33). His answer is, "No one!" because it's God himself who justifies us. And with that judgment comes all the infinite blessings God has stored up for his sons and daughters. The prize goes to Jesus and to those who belong to Jesus. For him it's earned but for us it's all grace.

Justification by faith isn't some legal fiction. It's not some abstract theological concept that never touches our lives. It's good news and it changes everything. Knowing that Jesus has delivered you out of the need to justify yourself sets you free to really live for God. Tim Keller says, "Do you realize that it is only in the gospel of Jesus Christ that you get the verdict before the performance? For the Buddhist . . . performance leads to the verdict. If you are a Muslim, performance leads to the verdict. All this means that every day you are in the courtroom, every day you are on trial. That is the problem. But Paul is saying that in Christianity the verdict leads to the performance. It is not the performance that leads to the verdict. In Christianity the moment we believe, God says, 'This is my beloved son in whom I am well pleased' . . . The verdict is in. And now I perform on the basis of the verdict. Because he loves me and accepts me."[5]

Unlike the older brother in the story of the prodigal son, Jesus doesn't point his finger and make a case for sending us away.

When we understand this it gives us a whole new lease on life. Milton says that when he realized the ramifications of what Jesus had done, "I felt like a kid in a candy store. How did I not see these things before? The gospel is the craziest thing I've ever heard in my life. And it's true!"[6]

Not only is it true, it liberates us to live for Jesus. Milton says that once he realized he was "released from the burden of having to maintain my righteous standing with God" he was fueled with energy to live for God. "I quickly found that I had enormous amounts of passion to put into . . . ministering God's amazing grace to other people. I had never had such energy available for ministry before because so much of it was consumed with tending to my own standing before God."[7]

As believers we need to know that we can stop tending to our standing before God. We can just take in what Jesus has done and make it the basis of our lives. We don't have to live trying to measure up to some phantom standard. We don't have to spend our energy trying to justify our existence. We can take our guilty consciences to Jesus and let him wash away our guilt and remind us that we don't go in and out of the Father's house based on our performance—we're in to stay because we're in him to stay.

As I've already said, I struggle with this. If I've really blown it the day before, argued with Charles, forgotten to do something I promised to do, backed into someone in the parking lot, I feel condemned. I can look at the day ahead and launch into life as if checking everything off my list is going to justify my existence. I can get all caught up in what people think of me, the impression I'm making, as if that's where the blessing comes from and how it gets taken away. I feel responsible for everything from my children's happiness to the weather. I can be super sensitive to criticism and live with that tight defensive attitude of needing to be right all the time.

Linda and I are very much alike in this. We call ourselves The Sisters of Perpetual Apology because we walk around feeling like we've done something wrong. We're sorry for the mistakes we made in raising our children, sorry for burning the dinner, sorry for what we said in that conversation we just had. We were in a Bible study where the speaker made passing mention of "that type of person who apologizes when you're the one who bumped into her." We both shrank down in our seats, convinced she was talking about us. There are lots of women who belong in this sisterhood, lots of women who need to know that Jesus has set us free so that we can live like The Sisters of Perpetual Blessing. We can bond together in gospel friendships and remind each other of the liberating truth of the gospel.

He's lived our life for us. He's delivered us out from under the need to justify our own existence. He's taken us into the Father's house where we can leave all the responsibility in our Father's hand and just boldly revel in his blessing. That's where the story has brought us as God's people. We can swing the weight of our lives entirely off ourselves and on to Jesus and then live for his glory.

The most awesome thing about the story of the prodigal son is how many roles Jesus plays. Not only is he the true older brother; he's the servant, the one who takes away our filthy clothes and dresses us in himself and places his ring of sonship on our finger and then slips our feet into his royal slippers. He's the one who serves us at the table. And even more amazing—he's the fatted calf. He died so we could feast on him. He's the bounty and the richness of our lives. Every role he plays in this story was prefigured or predicted long ago. Jesus has become a servant for our sakes so we can finally just relax and be the guest.

> "Love bade me welcome; yet my soul drew back,
>   Guilty of dust and sin.
> But quick-eyed Love, observing me grow slack
>   From my first entrance in,
> Drew nearer to me, sweetly questioning,
>   If I lacked anything.
> 'A guest,' I answered, 'worthy to be here.'
>   Love said, 'You shall be he.'
> 'I, the unkind, ungrateful: Ah, my dear,
>   I cannot look on thee.'
> Love took my hand, and smiling did reply,
>   'Who made the eyes but I?'
> 'Truth, Lord, but I have marred them; let my shame
>   Go where it doth deserve.'
> 'And know you not,' says Love, 'who bore the blame?'
>   'My dear, then I will serve.'
> 'You must sit down,' says Love, 'and taste my meat.'
>   So I did sit and eat."[8]

Notes

1. John Williamson Nevin, *The Mystical Presence* (Eugene, Ore.: Wipf and Stock, 2012), 156.

2. Milton Vincent, *A Gospel Primer* (Colorado Springs: Focus Publishing, 2008), 93.

3. Sydney Pollack, "Movies Justify My Existence," contactmovies.com, April 18 2005.

4. Timothy Keller, *The Freedom of Self-Forgetfulness* (Chorley, England: 10 Publishing, 2012), 22.

5. Ibid., 39.

6. Vincent, *Gospel Primer*, 96.

7. Ibid.,

8. George Herbert, *The Temple* (Brewster, Mass.: Paraclete Press, 2001), 194.

The Passing
of the Eclipse

It's the best of times and the worst of times, this stage in life when your children are giving birth to children and your parents are slowly going downhill. I (Charles) had kissed Janet goodbye at the Burbank airport where she'd caught a flight to Eugene, Oregon, to be with our daughter, Kate, whose contractions were coming on strong. She got there in time to hold Kate's hand in that hard moment when the doctor said the baby was under stress. She was with her when Kate was wheeled in for a C-section and she got to hold that miracle first grandchild, that Charlotte, just moments after she was born.

Meanwhile, I was on a flight back home to Oklahoma. After a long downward slide into dementia from Parkinson's disease, my father was slipping away. The doctor had called from my dad's bedside to tell me the end would be coming soon. He didn't recommend taking him to the hospital to die; there was no reason he couldn't stay right there at home where my stepmom had been caring for him with the help of aides for more long nights and hard days than I could imagine. I agreed and asked to speak to my dad. They held the phone to his ear and I felt compelled to say, "Dad, it's time. I think Jesus is calling you home." Out of his dementia I heard a response, a noise of agreement.

Ten minutes later he was gone. What I thought would be an urgent flight home to see him once more had become a trip with my son Peter to help to lay him in the grave and give thanks for his life.

I was thinking about my dad off and on as we flew. His oil-company job had kept him away from home for long stretches of time and after my mother died when I was eight and my brother was thirteen, life became pretty grim around our house. Still, I had a loving father although he came from a generation when love was unspoken between a father and a son. During those final years of illness the hardness I'd harbored against him softened and our bond of love was renewed, partly because I'd come to know my heavenly Father better. I could let my earthly father off the hook for not being perfect because I'd been learning what it means to live in my heavenly Father's house as his dearly loved son.

Matt Redman expressed this so powerfully when he visited the HAVEN studios. He told me about his own father and how he'd committed suicide when Matt was just a young boy. I was imagining what a deep mark of abandonment that must have left on his life. I started to sympathize but Matt said it was okay because he'd never lacked for a father's love. He hadn't known how his father died until his mother broke the news several years later. It was like losing his father all over again, but by then he was hearing another Father's song. He was hearing his heavenly Father singing a song of love over his life. It was out of this profound sense of being loved that he wrote "The Father's Song." He told me that on the day he recorded it, March 1, it suddenly struck him that this was his deceased father's birthday, that he would have been sixty years old on this very day. Matt realized what an amazing thing it was that he had never felt fatherless. He said he could listen to a lot of songs, a lot of messages coming at him, but the one he knew would impact his life more than any other was the "Father's Song."

The Father is singing his song of love over every one of his children but not all of us are hearing it. For some of us, our heavenly Father is a blank, a face we can't seem to see. We live like orphans, harassed and worn out by the requirements of life, because we have no sense of our Father's love.

Emily Dickinson described what it's like to live that way in a letter she wrote to her mentor, Thomas Wentworth Higginson. He had asked her to tell him about her daily life and if she had any companionship. She wrote back,

> You ask of my Companions—Hills, Sir, and the Sundown, and a Dog, large as myself, that my Father bought me. They are better than Beings. And the noise in the Pool at Noon excels my Piano. My Mother does not care for thought and Father, too busy with his Briefs to notice what we do. They are religious, except me, and they address an Eclipse, every morning whom they call their "Father."[1]

If you read Dickinson's poetry you can see how troubled she was by a looming sense of God's presence, a presence that always seemed to be haunting her life. At times she would rail at him for making her feel guilty; other times she would try to banish him from her mind so she could just revel in the hills and the sundown. For the poet, God's sun was blocked out.

For some of us God is like that. Jesus is wonderful—but the Father is a threat, often because we've had difficult relationships with our earthly fathers. Some have experienced much worse than indifference at the hands of their fathers. Yet we need to know where to look to see our Father's face and to understand his heart so the eclipse will pass away and the brilliance of his love will flood our hearts. If we want to see our Father, we need to look at Jesus.

"Show us the Father and that will be enough for us," Philip said to Jesus.

Jesus had been assuring them they didn't need to worry because there was a lot of room in the Father's house—and he was going there to prepare a place for them. But he was coming again. He was coming back to receive them to himself and they would be with him and the Father forever. Meanwhile, they knew the way to the Father.

The stress level in the room was rising with all this talk of departure; and the disciples were struggling really hard to understand what in the world Jesus was talking about. "We don't even know where you're going! How can we possibly know the way?" "Show us the Father and that will be enough for us."

Jesus entered into our pain with so much compassion it broke his heart.

Jesus was amazed by all this confusion. He said, "Don't you know me, Philip, even after I have been among you such a long time? Anyone who has seen me has seen the Father. How can you say, 'Show us the Father'?" Jesus was giving them, and us, the key to seeing the Father's face: just look at Jesus.

Earlier in John he said, "The Son can do nothing by himself; he can do only what he sees his Father doing, because whatever the Father does the Son also does" (John 5:19). If we think Jesus is the nice one and God the Father is the stern, unapproachable one, we need to understand what Jesus is saying. He's telling us that his heart and the Father's heart beat as one. Every gentle healing, every act of kindness, every word of love we see and hear from Jesus is coming out of the Father's heart. When we look at Jesus the shadow moves away from the sun, the revelation pours forth, and we see the face of God.

When Jesus' friend Lazarus died, his sisters Mary and Martha suffered tremendous anxiety, hoping Jesus would arrive in time to heal him. When he didn't, they were heartbroken. But as Philip Ryken says,

No one suffered more than Jesus. We see this in the way he relates to Mary: "When Jesus saw her weeping, and the Jews who had come with her also weeping, he was deeply moved in his spirit and greatly troubled" . . . the vocabulary here indicates extremely intense emotion. The sadness Jesus felt for this loss and his rage against the horrors of death came from the depths of his soul . . . "Jesus wept" and the reason for (his) tears were not lost on his fellow mourners, who said, "See how he loved him."[2]

Jesus entered into our pain with so much compassion it broke his heart. But he wants us to understand that this is also our Father's compassion. He does not want us to miss this so before he raised Lazarus from the dead he prayed, "Father, I thank you that you have heard me. I knew that you always hear me, but I said this for the benefit of the people standing here, that they may believe that you sent me."

We can see our Father's face in Jesus—in his compassion, his kindness, his willingness to feed, and heal, and teach but we can see it most clearly on the cross. That's where the full force of our Father's love comes blazing forth. When Jesus was in the upper room talking to his disciples he told them, "If you really know me, you will know my Father as well. From now on, you do know him and have seen him."

The disciples knew Jesus, of course. They'd been with him for three years, day in and day out. But he was telling them that they would finally really know both him and the Father—when they saw him on the cross. He was telling them, "When you see my love poured out with nothing held back you will be seeing your Father's love poured out with nothing held back. Look at me on the cross and know that you're seeing your Father's heart. See it beating with love, tearing down barriers, creating peace. Let it come into your darkness and take away the eclipse. See the passionate love of your Father giving up his Son for you. See the lengths he was willing to go to clear the way and bring you close, lengths you could never have conceived in a million years."

One of the most memorable moments of our life happened one night when a friend showed up unannounced at our door and told us he'd finally seen it. We'd been leading a Sunday school class about the fatherhood of God, but there was one man, an elder in the church, who just couldn't get hold of it. But that night the doorbell rang and when we opened it there he stood with tears running down his face.

"Is it really true? Is it true that I don't have to earn my Father's approval? I've been doing that my entire life with my earthly father. I've never been able to please him but I just keep trying even though he's been dead for over ten years. Is it true that I don't have to do that anymore?"

He was seeing his heavenly Father's face for the first time. Of course we invited him in and offered him dessert and assured him that it was really true but he already knew—and it was the cross that did it. He finally understood that his Father loved him so much he'd given up his Son. He realized the cross was his Father's welcome home, his Father's open arms, running toward him with no reproach, no conditions, nothing but deep delight. He realized in the depths of his soul that his Father was already pleased with him in Jesus.

Some seven hundred years before it happened Isaiah wrote a detailed explanation of why the Messiah had to suffer and a graphic description of how bad it would be. But one chapter later God described the unbelievable take-away value of that suffering for us. He said it meant that he would never be angry with us again. It meant he would never rebuke us again. In his deep compassion he had cleared all our disqualification out of the way so he could bring us home. That was what this elder finally understood and he was weeping with relief and joy because of it.

"When you see me you've seen the Father." We can look at Jesus and see what our Father was willing to do so we could become his sons and daughters. John says that Jesus gives everyone who receives him, "the right to become children of God—children born not of natural descent, nor of human decision or a husband's will, but born of God." We're so used to calling God "our Father" that we often don't realize that this is only possible because of Jesus. We can miss how breathtaking it is that we're his children, that God sent Jesus into the world so we could have "the right to become the children of God," children who can address him not just as "God" or "Allah" or "Yahweh," but as "our Father"—"our Abba."

Bilquis Sheikh tells in her autobiography how this stunning realization completely changed her life. She was born in 1912 in northern Pakistan, and raised a Muslim in an elite family with a long history of political power and great wealth. Bilquis herself was well known and highly respected throughout the country, but when her husband divorced her she went into seclusion. Eventually she started reading the Qur'an for solace but didn't find what she looking for, although she noticed the name of Jesus cropping up now and then. She began to wonder what the Christian Scriptures taught and eventually asked her Christian chauffeur to bring her a Bible.

The first verse that caught her eye was Romans 9:25–26, "I will call them 'my people' who are not my people; and I will call her 'my loved one' who is not my loved one. . . . In the very place where it was said to them, 'You are not my people,' there they will be called 'children of the living God.'"

It left her confused but strangely excited. Who was God? Was he the God of the Qur'an she'd heard about all her life, or was he this entirely different God of grace? The distress of not knowing finally drove her to her knees, "Which one is your book?"[3] she prayed. The answer came gently, "In which book do you meet me as your Father?"[4] God was telling her that she could believe what she was reading in the New

Testament, that it wasn't blasphemy—the Holy God actually did want her to call him Father.

As a Muslim she had always thought of God as one solid solitary being, but God continued to break into her life in profound and miraculous ways until she finally understood that he was a trinity of persons, Father, Son, and Spirit, and that each one had a role in bringing her into this new relationship.

The Trinity is a mystery. This unified, three-person God goes far beyond the capacities of our finite minds but this much we can understand: At the center of the universe there is a relationship. God is not just one person who existed all by himself until he created someone to love. God is not Unitarian; he's Trinitarian, which means from all eternity there's always been a relationship of love. If God is Trinitarian then "the deepest mystery of his being God is an intimate relationship, a fellowship, a community of love."[5] Augustine put it like this in the fifth century, "God is (all at once) Lover, Beloved, and Love itself."[6]

It is an awesome thing to be able to say "our Father" to the living God.

The Old Testament hinted at this multiplicity and oneness of God but when Jesus came the sun broke through. We could finally see God as he is: Father, Son, and Holy Spirit. Now imagine that the Father desires with all of his heart for us to be included in that circle of love. Imagine the Son sharing his Father's passion for that to happen. Imagine him taking on our flesh and blood so he wouldn't be ashamed to call us his brothers and sisters. Imagine him enduring unimaginable suffering to remove our disqualification so we too could become the sons of God. Imagine him taking our alien nature into himself so it could be put to death and we could be born again in him and share his nature.

Imagine him rising from the grave exultant that it was done, that he had made us his brothers and sisters. Imagine him meeting Mary in the garden and telling her, "Go instead to my brothers and tell them that I am ascending to my Father and your Father, to my God and your God." Imagine that fifty days later the Father poured the "Spirit of Sonship" into the hearts of his children so they could call him "Abba."

Now you can stop imagining because that's what happened. That's the jaw-dropping surprise of the story. That's what Bilquis came to understand. We can call him "Father" because Jesus has brought us into the relationship of love that he has always had with the Father, and the Spirit brings that relationship into our hearts. As a former Muslim she knew what we so often miss—that it is an awesome thing to be able to say "our Father" to the living God. We can let the words roll off our tongues without realizing what an unimaginable privilege it is to say them. As Dale Bruner says in his Matthew commentary, "We will never be able to calculate the honor that has been done us by being allowed to say, 'Our Father.'"[7]

Jesus not only wants us to know we have this intimacy, he wants us to see how it changes the way we pray. He tells us, "Don't pray like the Pharisees and the hypocrites." They weren't really praying at all, according to Jesus; they were just putting on a religious show to impress other people. We lose intimacy with our Father when we get full of ourselves like that.

I (Charles) was good friends with the late Bible teacher and pastor James Montgomery Boice and often heard him tell a story that gets this across so clearly. He and a friend made a trip around the Mediterranean that eventually brought them to Egypt and the great temple of Luxor built more than three thousand years ago by Amenophis III. As they were looking up in awe at the soaring columns, they happened to notice that perched on the very top of one of them was a small house. Their guide explained that a farmer living in the area had scratched about in the sand, found what he thought was bedrock, and built his house on top of it. But then the archeologists came, the excavation began, and it turned out what he thought was bedrock was actually the summit of one of those huge temple columns. Eventually his little house was way up high, eighty feet in the air.

It can happen to us in a heartbeat, being isolated because we think we're something big and important. We hear a compliment and suddenly we're way up high on a pedestal, far away from the heart of God. Jesus is telling us to come down, to leave the arena of human approval, to humble ourselves and enter that intimate place, that closet, where we can be completely alone with our Father. He said the Pharisees had their reward; they had the applause, the honor, the admiration of the crowds; but we could have the true reward, the one the Father gives us. We could have the sweet delight of being in his presence and hearing his song of love.

Jesus also tells us not to pray like the pagans. The pagans pray to someone they don't know—and they don't know if he's listening. They try to get their needs met by saying a lot of words and performing a lot of rituals. It's a little shocking to realize that when we do that, when we monologue to God without really being sure if he's hearing us, we're actually praying like a pagan. It's also a little shocking to realize that some churches are starting to incorporate straight-up pagan practices into their worship.

We saw it firsthand when we were staying in a little village in England and decided to go to the evensong service. We entered this centuries old Norman-era church and up in the chancel were about eight people sitting in a circle. We were warmly welcomed and given a seat and within few minutes the service began. There was a short homily about how our lives are like a landscape. It wasn't exactly clear to us what it was about, but England has a way of instilling niceness in you so we just sat there smiling back at the lovely people. But then the priest gave us each a piece of paper with concentric circles drawn on it and the words "I AM" written in the inner circle. We were supposed to fill in each of the circles with truth about ourselves until we reached the inner circle and discovered our oneness with the "I AM." We recognized it as an Eastern meditation technique that supposedly centers you inward so you can see that all is one and therefore all are divine. We politely excused ourselves and left.

Pagans look for God in all the wrong places but we don't have to. We have this tremendously privileged place of direct fellowship with the living God. It takes two for fellowship so it's really good news to discover that we're not god after all, because otherwise there would be no face filled with love to look at, no give-and-take relationship of love with the One who created us. Jesus wants us to know that this is what we have in him and that we can simply talk to our Father as a child would. We can rest in trust that our Father is taking care of us and ask him for the things we need and know that he'll answer.

I (Janet) started praying a few years back that I could know my heavenly Father better. I knew he had adopted me and that I was a full-fledged child of God. In most cultures it's the sons who have the privileged status; they take pride of place in their parents' hearts, they carry on their father's business, they retain his name, and they get the inheritance. Daughters don't rate. But in Christ all believers regardless of gender are equally the sons of God. We all have the exact same identity and privileges and relationship with our heavenly Father because we're all united to Jesus.

In Christ Jesus you are all children of God through faith, for all of you who were baptized into Christ have clothed yourselves with Christ. There is neither Jew nor Gentile, neither slave nor free, nor is there male and female, for you are all one in Christ Jesus. (Galatians 3:26–28)

I knew this good news. I knew I was forgiven and justified and adopted and provided for but I didn't feel as if I knew my Father personally. I wanted that communion John Owens describes as "a taste of his sweetness."

When I read Jean Webster's classic novel *Daddy-Long-Legs* a few years ago I thought, "This really captures the longing I have for a close connection with my heavenly Father." It's the story of Jerusha Abbott, who was the oldest orphan in the orphanage. Every Wednesday when the trustees came to visit she had to wipe the noses of the other ninety-seven orphans and make sure they were starched and presentable. One Wednesday after being on her feet since five in the morning, "doing everybody's bidding," she was leaning against the window watching the carriages leave, following them in her imagination to the big houses on the hillside.[8] She was just thinking what it would be like to be able to say "home," when her daydreams were interrupted by a summons to the matron's office.

Thankfully, instead of the reprimand she was expecting, Mrs. Lippet gave her a piece of good news. One of the trustees had decided to pay her way to college. His monetary provision was very generous, too generous in Matron's opinion, but he did have two stipulations: she was never to know his name and she was required to write him a long letter every week. Jerusha had almost caught a glimpse of her benefactor as she was coming into Matron's office and he was leaving, but she only saw his elongated shadow against the wall. From then on she referred to him as "Daddy-Long-Legs."

That pretty well sums up how I felt about my heavenly Father. He provides everything I need, and I'm supposed to communicate with him, but I don't really know who he is. I know Jesus, but the Father is just a shadow.

Then Charles and I were staying in a cabin for a few days of rest and on the counter was a guest log where former visitors had written down their thoughts. One entry said, "My life changed when I realized what was in the heart of God toward me." I read those words and it was like a lightbulb of realization flashed in my brain. I thought, "I keep sighing and thinking I don't know what's in my Father's heart toward me; but I do. I know it from Jesus. He hasn't withheld his name—he's blazed it forth. He's looked at me face to face in love and told me to call him 'Abba.'"

Shortly after that a friend recommended a book by John Owen where he talks about the unique communion we have with each member of the Trinity. He writes, "The chief way by which the saints have communion with the Father is love—free, undeserved, eternal love. This love the Father pours on the saints. Saints are to see God as full of love to them."[9] When I read that I determined to just start doing it, to start seeing God that way, to believe it and give him thanks for it. Before long the reality of it began to fill my heart. I started to hear the Father singing his song of love.

We take everything from our Father and then we give our love back to him in joy.

Owen says, "The greatest sorrow and burden you can lay on the Father, the greatest unkindness you can do to him, is not to believe that he loves you."[10] I had never thought about it that way before. Communion is a mutual exchange. "Our communion with God lies in his giving himself to us and our giving ourselves . . . to him."[11] When I don't take time to have that communion my world loses its center and its delight and I revert to functioning like an orphan. But when I spend time with my Father, when I listen to his song and then *sing one back to him,* that's when I come home. That's communion. Communion is both—taking and giving. We take everything from our Father and then we give our love back to him in joy.

God has adopted us in Jesus and we will never be able to calculate the honor—but we can take time to ruminate on it. We can pause and focus on the stunning fact that we can say "our Father" because God has made us his sons in Jesus. We can spend time in that private communion only we who know Jesus can have with our Father God. We can think about what an all-consuming joy it is to Jesus that he has brought us into his sonship and how glad it makes him when we live it out. Every word he spoke and everything he did was focused on making that happen. He lived his entire life showing us what it means to be a son of God—not in some ethereal sense that we can't get hold of but right here where we live.

Jesus brought his sonship into our world and lived it out among us; he showed us firsthand the down to earth ramifications of living as the sons of God in a world where, as he said, every day has enough trouble of its own so we don't have to borrow any from tomorrow. We live in a broken place but we don't live here as unloved orphans who have to fend for ourselves. We live here as sons of the living God. God takes us in his arms and comforts us with his love and reassures us that we're not on our own anymore. We're not orphans. Jesus spent a lot of time explaining this:

"Look at the birds of the air; they do not sow or reap or store away in barns, and yet your heavenly Father feeds them. Are you not much more valuable than they?" (Matthew 6:26)

"Do not be afraid, little flock, for your Father has been pleased to give you the kingdom." (Luke 12:32)

Jesus wants us to know that our Father watches over every hair on our head. We can trust him to protect us in the safety of his good and perfect will, to be constantly attentive to our needs, to provide for us and carry us with a tender, protective compassion for our weakness. We can come to him in our total incapacity and ask for his total help knowing that he has the same tender heart toward us that we have toward our own helpless children. "If you then, though you are evil, know how to give good gifts to your children, how much more will your Father in heaven give the Holy Spirit to those who ask him!"

A good friend of ours finally realized this at a prayer retreat we were on together. The leader told us to spend some quiet time meditating on how we thought of God and where that perception comes from. Our friend told us that as he thought back on his childhood he realized his dad would often send him off with a task to do and when he brought it back for his approval tell him it wasn't quite right and send him off again. He didn't feel like his father ever approved of what he did, that he never got it right, and he'd transferred that scenario to his relationship with God. What a joyous thing it was when the light poured into his heart and he realized his heavenly Father isn't like that. He isn't sending him off to do things on his own; he's given him the Spirit. Not only that, his heavenly Father delights in everything he does in obedience to him, regardless of how imperfect it might be.

Our Father will give us everything good there is to give. Even if we don't have much in this world, even if we suffer in this world because of Jesus, we can stand up tall and rejoice because we're the heirs of God. "Do not be afraid, little flock, for your Father has been pleased to give you the kingdom." Believe it! The kingdom of God and everything in it belongs to you. The new heavens and the new earth, which will one day be filled with the knowledge of God, belong to you. That's the story. The Father has flung the door wide open in Jesus and revealed his face of love to us. And right now he's reshaping us, in love, in the image of his Son.

Notes

1. Lisa Grunwalk and Stephen Adler, *Women's Letters: America from the Revolutionary War to the Present* (New York: Random House: 2008), 288.

2. Philip Ryken, *Loving the Way Jesus Loves* (Wheaton: Crossway, 2012), 86.

3. Bilquis Sheikh, *I Dared to Call Him Father* (Grand Rapids: Baker Book House, 1978), 53.

4. Ibid.

5. Darrell Johnson, *Experiencing the Trinity* (Vancouver, BC: Regent College Publishing, 2002), 51.

6. Ibid., 51.

7. Frederick Dale Bruner, *The Christ Book* (Grand Rapids: Eerdmans, 2004), 295.

8. Jean Webster, *Daddy-Long-Legs* (New York: Penguin Books, 2004 ed.), 5.

9. John Owen, *Communion with God* (The Banner of Truth Trust, 1991), 12.

10. Ibid., 13.

11. Ibid., 3.

The Great Dilemma

An avid golfing friend of ours has a favorite story he loves to tell. It happened when he was teeing up at the first hole on a course he'd never played before. He carefully placed his ball, got into his very best golfer's stance, eyed the green, and swung. As the ball went sailing off into the rough he heard a loud, raspy voice behind him say, "Oh no!"

He and the friend he was playing with both looked around but there was no one there—just a big black raven sitting on the branch of a tree. They shrugged, and his friend teed up and took his first swing. Just as he hit the ball, sure enough the raven cawed out, "Oh no!" At the end of the round back at the clubhouse they asked if they were dreaming or if there really was a raven offering unsolicited commentary on the first hole.

Everyone laughed. Apparently he'd been hanging out in that tree for a couple of years and had heard so many golfers say, "Oh no" he'd learned to say it himself.

Sometimes the Christian life can feel like one "oh no" after another, especially when we've been walking down the road awhile. We think we ought to be getting better by now—but instead we just keep hitting the ball into the rough. We know Jesus died for us, that we've been adopted, and that we're meant to be living like the sons and daughters of God, but we feel a little like a frustrated golfer whose game just never seems to improve even after years of trying. In fact, we might actually be getting worse.

We came across something C. S. Lewis wrote in a journal that gets to the very heart of our problem. It was written when he was a young man and still an atheist, which makes his insight even more remarkable. It was his practice in those pre-Christian days to record not only his daily activities but his musings about the books he was reading. His choice of reading material was surprisingly broad, including not only great works of English literature but a wide range of other things as well. In one entry, after he'd just finished a biography of a Christian woman named Hannah More, he made this observation: "You see the self examination taking a form in which it is bound to become worse and worse: the more you scratch the more you itch. The problem raised is this: how to be seriously concerned with goodness without letting the 'empirical ego' become the absorbing object. Perhaps it is insoluble."[1]

> *Just when we think we've conquered some sin, pride grows back in its place.*

Lewis zeroed in on the great dilemma of the Christian life. We become "seriously concerned with goodness" but we can't seem to walk down that road without falling into a pit. We try hard to live the Christian life but the more we try the more tangled up in ourselves we get. In Lewis' opinion that's what happened to Hannah More. The more she tried to be holy the more self-focused she became.

Augustine called it *incurvatas in se*—the inward curvature of our hearts. We head off in the direction of virtue, but our egos exert such a strong gravitational pull we curve back on ourselves. We can't seem to escape our orbit around our selves. Luther defined sin as "the self turned in on itself," and we groan with the truth of it. Just when we're making a little progress in the right direction, what do we do but step aside and start admiring ourselves in the mirror?

Lewis discovered this almost immediately after he came to faith. It was easy to be detached and critical as a young atheist; now he was a Christian and he had to be "seriously concerned with goodness." Within a few months he found himself snared by the same "insoluble" problem he had so callously observed in Hannah More. He described the struggle in a letter he wrote to his old friend Arthur Greeves:

> During my afternoon "meditations"—which I at least attempt quite regularly now—I have found out ludicrous and terrible things about my own character. Sitting by, watching the rising thoughts to break their necks as they pop up, one learns to know the sort of thoughts that do come. And, will you believe it, one out of every three is the thought of self-admiration: when everything else fails, having had its neck broken, up comes the thought "what an admirable fellow I am to have broken their necks!" I catch myself posturing before the mirror, so to speak, all day long. I pretend I am carefully thinking out what to say to the next pupil (for his good, of course) and then suddenly realize I am really thinking how frightfully clever I'm going to be and how he will admire me. . . . And then when you force yourself to stop it, you admire yourself for doing that. It is like fighting the hydra. . . . There seems to be no end to it. Depth under depths of self-love and self-admiration.[2]

Lewis's thoughts were like the many-headed hydra in Greek mythology that couldn't be defeated because every time you cut off one of its heads two more grew back in its place. Lewis had the keen insight to see that the heads that grew back were worse than the ones he cut off. Just when we think we've conquered some sin, pride grows back in its place.

We can take solace in the fact that nobody understood this problem better than the apostle Paul, and no one was more convinced that we have an answer to it in Jesus. In Romans 7 he describes how much we want to be transformed and all the efforts we make to bring it about in ourselves and how we inevitably end up worse than when we started. He uses the word "I" ("ego" in Greek) nine different times. He seems to be hammering away at the fact that if it's up to us it's not going to happen. At the end of his long description of this struggle to keep God's law he cries out, "What a wretched man I am! Who will rescue me from this body that is subject to death?" And then he supplies the answer to his own question, "Thanks be to God, who delivers me through Jesus Christ our Lord!"

Before Christ, scrupulous law-keeping had been Paul's all-consuming passion. His great ambition was to become the premier up-and-coming young Jew, the one who excelled everyone else in his zeal to keep the traditions of his people. Some of us can identify with that. We want to be the best Christian around. In Philippians he lists all the righteousness he'd chalked up on his résumé: "circumcised on the eighth day, of the people of Israel, of the tribe of Benjamin, a Hebrew of Hebrews; in regard to the law, a Pharisee; as for zeal, persecuting the church; as for righteousness based on the law, faultless."

But did you notice how he put "persecuting the church" right in the middle of his righteousness résumé? Why did he throw this great negative in with all those things that sound so positive? He was being ironic. He was making the point that having what he calls "a righteousness of my own" had ended up making him hostile to other people. That's what self-righteousness does. It draws a line in our hearts and says, "We're the good guys and they're the bad guys." Some of us can identify with that attitude, too. We're sure we're right and we've gone into battle with the people we're convinced are wrong.

Saul was convinced the Christians were wrong because, after all, the law clearly says, "Cursed is anyone who hangs on a tree" (see Deut. 21:23), and Jesus had been very publicly crucified, literally hung on a tree. His followers had to be stamped out for the sake of the nation. Saul was sure he was the man for the job. He and his cohorts were on their way to Damascus to do exactly that when suddenly, out of nowhere, a brilliant light appeared and he heard a voice. It was the voice of the One who was going to solve the insoluble dilemma of his life:

"Saul, Saul, why do you persecute me?"

Saul knew the Scriptures. Nobody knew them better. He knew what it was like to come into the presence of the living God and he realized it was happening to him at that very moment. It's hard to imagine what might have been going through his mind but whatever it was it came out as an urgent question, "Who are you, Lord?" The answer came back, "I am Jesus, whom you are persecuting."

If there was ever a courtroom moment this should have been it. Yet Saul seemed to know that Jesus wasn't there to condemn him. He was there to call him. Later when he described what happened that day he simply said, "God revealed his Son in me." He realized this encounter was a devastating act of sheer grace. He who least deserved it was being co-opted by the Messiah and his response was to immediately and wholeheartedly submit to Jesus. "What should I do, Lord?" It had to be the quickest one-eighty in history.

Paul often told the story of his traumatically beautiful encounter with Jesus to illustrate the humbling effect the gospel is meant to have in every believer's life. His righteousness was completely stripped away and he became a profoundly humbled man who was deeply in love with Jesus. "He loved me and gave himself for me." Paul couldn't get over it.

The gospel puts an end to our struggle for righteousness by showing us we don't have any in ourselves, not at the beginning of our Christian life and not at the end of it, either. We can just give it up because we're not making a shot that goes into the rough now and then—we're completely void of the life of God. We are "self turned in on itself." But praise be to God we can turn away from ourselves and look to Jesus and receive our life from him. Our Father has provided a way out of our great dilemma—a way for us to be re-created in the image of his Son.

Years back we went to a weeklong conference in Pensacola, Florida. There were several highly credentialed Christian speakers and the content was rich but at this point in our lives we don't remember very much of what was said. All the copious notes we took are probably yellowing in a cardboard box in the garage somewhere or more likely lost in one of our many moves. But there was one singular moment we've never lost. It happened right in the middle of one of the lectures. A young woman walked up behind the man who was speaking and just stood there. She was wearing one of the official badges of a volunteer from the host church and from the strained look on her face you could tell she was waiting for a pause so she could say something important. The speaker couldn't see her but the rest of us could, and eventually he realized our attention had been diverted to something behind his back. He frowned and turned around and when he saw her standing there just erupted with annoyance.

"What is it?!"

She cringed and told him, "I'm sorry but there's an emergency message for someone and it can't wait."

He gave her the microphone, she announced the name, the person got up and hurried out, and the speaker turned back to face us. The room got very quiet. He just stood there for a moment and then he said, "Now you have seen what is in me. Now you know why I need Jesus." That moment illustrated the power of the gospel more than all the words that were spoken that week. Only the gospel can humble us. Only the gospel can put to death the hydra head of pride because only the gospel sets us free us to confess our pride.

I (Charles) was having a discussion recently with a friend about how we wanted to communicate the gospel. We both agreed it was tempting to tell stories where we come out looking good, where we're the heroes—but neither of us wanted to do that. We wanted to tell stories where Jesus is the hero. We wanted to glorify him. My friend said to me, "Well, one thing for sure, when we talk about Jesus we have a lot more material to work with." That's what the gospel is meant to do. It's meant to cut us deeply, right to the core, and take away our self-admiration. It's meant to show us how foolish we are when we think we're heroes. It's meant to turn our attention away from ourselves and on to Jesus so we can fill up on his material.

There's some debate about whether Paul was describing his life before he was a Christian or afterwards in Romans 7, but it really doesn't matter. What matters is that all his efforts to change himself convinced him that the only thing operating in him was death. But it was all good because that very realization opened his heart to receive the answer God provided. He could look away from himself to Jesus. We can do that too. We can identify with his struggle and learn its lesson and then turn our eyes to Jesus. We can throw all our self-righteousness away and say with Paul, "Thanks be to God, who delivers me through Jesus Christ our Lord!"

It's hard to throw our self-righteousness away—especially if we think we've chalked up some points. We need to be honest about that. It can feel a lot like death. On our mission trip to London we were having lunch with a lovely Hindu woman whose face was suffused with sublimity as she told us about giving her entire birthday meal to the poor without taking a bite for herself. We expressed our admiration but then Janet asked her, "Do you find that your good deeds have a tendency to turn into pride? Because that's what happens to me." Janet didn't realize how tactless her question was until she saw the anger in the woman's face. We don't like to have our righteousness threatened. When the Moravian Christians told John Wesley that the gospel required him to empty his hands of all his good deeds he was appalled. "What?" he said. "Will you rob me of my doings?" He felt like his very identity was being erased, like someone was stealing the treasure he'd worked so hard to store up over the years. But he came to see that it was worth it to have Jesus. When that man at the conference had his pride exposed it was a wrenchingly painful moment— but it was worth it because it allowed us all to see Jesus.

Paul was totally clear that self-righteousness and pride have to go if we want to have Jesus. The accomplishments that filled his résumé as a young man started to smell like excrement after he met the Lord— that's his word for it. He just threw them away in order to "gain Christ and be found in him." You can feel the draw the Lord exerted on his heart when he talks about the "surpassing value of knowing Christ Jesus my Lord." It's like a sweet perfume. For him it was more than worth it to trade off his own righteousness for "that which is through faith in Christ—the righteousness that comes from God on the basis of faith."

That same message of faith runs all through Paul's letters. Faith isn't a virtue to Paul. It's a Copernican revolution. Faith is making Jesus the consuming object. Faith is admitting we have no virtue and ascribing it all to Jesus. Faith is getting our life from Jesus.

We can easily turn faith into a work; into something we have to do. Our *incurvatas in se* always tends to take us back to ourselves. But faith is the anti-work. When the people asked Jesus, "What must we do to do the works God requires?" he told them, "The work of God is this: to believe in the one he has sent." That's where the story was headed all along. One failure after another just kept proving the point that the dilemma was truly unsolvable if it was up to us to solve. And when the final evidence was in, when the people of God were expelled from the Promised Land because of their massive failure to be his people, God made another covenant—a new covenant—where he promised to do it all so his people could live by faith.

Faith is a way of life—the Christian way of life—and for Paul it was the ultimate freedom. To move away from it back to yourself is the most profoundly foolish thing a person can do. Why would you do it? "Who has bewitched you?" Paul asked the Galatians. They were thinking of getting themselves circumcised; they were trying to locate their righteousness in themselves, in their flesh, and Paul couldn't imagine why they would even consider it. What were they thinking? Why in the world would they revert to that old do-it-yourself way of life—that failed way of life—when God had united them to Jesus? All through the letter he alternates between warnings about the danger of moving away from faith and great massive affirmations of what God has given them in Christ.

He warns them that if they move away from faith and turn back to themselves they'll be deserting the One who called them. They'll be saying that Christ died for nothing. They'll be trading in their life of freedom for a life of slavery. They'll be kissing their joy goodbye. They'll start biting and devouring each other. Worst of all, they'll end up missing Jesus. "Mark my words . . . Christ will be of no value to you!"

Faith is not just the way we get in the door; it's how we're meant to live our lives.

At the same time Paul reminds them of what happened when they first heard the gospel, how all they had to do was look to Jesus on the cross and trust in him and—what happened? God poured out his Spirit; he recreated them by uniting them to Jesus; he adopted them as his own sons and daughters through the redemption that came through Jesus; he shared the inheritance of his Son with them. Massive gifts of God and none of them came because they kept the Law—they all came by faith. They started their Christian life with faith and they were meant to keep living it by faith—to keep on receiving their life from Jesus.

For those of us who've been Christians a long time this can be like hearing the gospel all over again. It was for us. To realize we can turn away from ourselves to Jesus—to understand that faith is not just the way we get in the door, that it's how we're meant to live our lives—was tremendously liberating. It's such good news to know that we can just humble ourselves and give it up and receive our life from him, especially when we've reached the point where we've thrown down our clubs in frustration after a thousand "oh no's." And really, in our experience, we keep reaching that point again and again, because pride is the ultimate head of the hydra that only the gospel can put to death. But there's great relief in being humbled and great joy in turning to Jesus and making him the "absorbing object."

Lewis himself came to understand that this was God's great answer to his "insoluble" problem. In *Mere Christianity* he wrote,

> We must go from being confident about our efforts to the state in which we despair of doing anything for ourselves and leave it to God. I know the words "leave it to God" can be misunderstood. The sense in which a Christian leaves it to God is that he puts all his trust in Christ, trusts that Christ will share with him the perfect human obedience which he carried out from his birth to his crucifixion; that Christ will make us more like himself. In Christian language, he will share his "sonship" with us. He will make us "sons of God." Christ offers us something for nothing. He even offers us everything for nothing. In a sense the whole Christian life consists in accepting that very remarkable offer.[3]

Jesus offers himself for nothing. He makes us one with himself and he does it freely and completely. He wants us as close to him as we can be and there's no greater closeness than union. John Owen says, "Precious and excellent as Christ is, he becomes ours. He makes himself available to us with all his graces."[4] Faith is simply accepting that very remarkable offer. We can just admit we have no life in ourselves; we can repent again and again and do it freely, because we've been united to Christ. Thanks be to God, there's a way out of ourselves. As Paul puts it in Galatians, "I no longer live, but Christ lives in me. The life I now live in the body, I live by faith in the Son of God, who loved me and gave himself for me." The way he lives in us is by his Spirit.

Notes

1. C. S. Lewis, *All My Road Before Me* (Orlando: Harcourt Brace Jovanovich: 1991), 396.

2. Alan Jacobs, *The Narnian* (New York: HarperCollins: 2005), 133.

3. C. S. Lewis, *Mere Christianity* (New York: HarperCollins: 1980), 146–47.

4. John Owen, *Communion with God* (Carlisle, Pa.: The Banner of Truth Trust: 1991), 58.

7

Keeping in Step

We were at our daughter and son-in-law's house for Christmas when I (Charles) hit the proverbial wall. Janet had been looking forward to Christmas for weeks. She and Kate had spent long hours on the phone making lists and planning menus. I'd been too busy with the hectic year-end Christmas crunch of ministry to think about our personal celebration. In fact, I still had a ministry to-do list a mile long when we loaded up the packages and made the two-day drive north, with the weather getting worse by the mile.

By the time we arrived I was getting sick but I couldn't stop; I had to keep writing and recording Haven programs for the following week. While everyone else was being festive downstairs, baking and laughing and playing games, I was off in an upstairs bedroom pushing through. Two little granddaughters were bidding for my attention and I was upset that I couldn't spend time with them. Janet kept sticking her head in the door and whispering that my absence was putting a damper on things; that I should come be part of the family. My stress level was going through the roof. I was a sick, sour grump that Christmas, and Janet was really put out with me.

Thankfully we managed to get through Christmas Day without a major blowup and were packed and on the road the following morning just before dawn. Snow and sleet were steadily falling, as they had been for more than a week. As I gripped the steering wheel I was thinking to myself, "Perfect, the weather is just as miserable as I am." I was pretty sure Janet was going to start telling me how I'd ruined Christmas for everybody and I was going to get mad and tell her she didn't have any sympathy for my situation. To keep that conversation from happening I switched on a CD of Dr. Gordon Fee's lectures on the book of Galatians.

We were planning to take his two-week class at Regent College the following summer, so to bone up we'd ordered the CD ahead of time. The introductory lecture had taken us up to Kate's house and now we were into the second one. Gordon was saying that Paul mentions the Holy Spirit at least eighteen times in Galatians. It was more than I had ever realized. I'd always thought Galatians was mostly about justification. It wasn't long before Gordon left his academic tone and started preaching. I don't remember his exact words but the gist of it was: "Paul keeps repeating—you have the Spirit, you're Spirit-people and there are only two ways you can live: You can live *kata sarka*—according to the flesh—or you can live *kata pneuma*—according to the Spirit." Then he raised his voice and with gusto said, "Believers! We can live *kata pneuma!*"

I can still remember the moment his words broke through to me. It was just as the sun rose and broke through the clouds and the freezing mix stopped falling.

That was the Christmas I learned firsthand just how right Jesus was when he said, "Apart from me you can do nothing." I was at that very teachable moment when I could say with every ounce of my being, "Amen to that, Lord." I'd seen the ugliness of my own stressed-out, overtaxed self, and being in that place allowed me to really hear what Gordon was saying. It was such very good news to know that I wasn't doomed to live *kata sarka*, that I don't have to slug it out on my own, that the Father has sent the Spirit—and that the Spirit is the life of Jesus in me.

Jesus wants us to know that we have the Spirit. In that long talk he gave in the upper room he keeps referring to the coming of the Spirit. His disciples are about to enter that age between his ascension into heaven and his future return, and he wants them—and us—to know that we haven't been left to our own devices. He gives us the deeply compassionate reassurance, "I will ask the Father, and he will give you another advocate to help you and be with you forever—the Spirit of truth. The world cannot accept him, because it neither sees him nor knows him. But you know him, for he lives with you and will be in you."

When Jesus said the Spirit was "another advocate" he obviously meant someone other than himself. He was leaving to return to his Father but he would send another advocate just like himself. At first this sounds like a pretty bad trade-off, like someone saying, "Don't worry, son, I can't take you to the ballgame but I'll send my assistant." We want to say, "Jesus, please, we don't want another advocate—we want you!" But Jesus immediately reassures us, "I will not leave you as orphans; I will come to you."

The coming of the Spirit is the coming of Jesus not just to be with us but *in* us. He is, as Paul says, the "Spirit of the Christ" and he is living in us. As far as I can tell, walking in the Spirit means living in dependent fellowship with Jesus. We can rejoice in his closeness. We can delight in his presence. We can abide in his love. We can drink from his well. And we can continually rely on him to give us him-self—because he continually does. He gives us his life at just those points where we realize we need him, and after a while we realize we need him all the time.

At eighteen months of age I had polio. It happened right at the end of an epidemic that swept the globe and just before the development of the Salk vaccine that brought it to an end. The doctors told my parents I would never be able to walk and might possibly live the remainder of my life in an iron lung. By God's grace I can breathe on my own and, though I walk with a limp, I can walk. But living in this post-polio body means I experience physical weakness every day. I have no choice but to depend on the Lord to give me strength. But my spiritual weakness is even more profound than the weakness I feel in my limbs. I don't pretend to know all that much about living *kata pneuma* but I know it means I can depend on the Lord to pour out his power on to my weakness. The simple realization that I have the Spirit and that I can rely on him makes all the difference.

> *Jesus never, ever thinks selfishly; he gives himself to us all the time.*

Paul seems to have operated on this basis all the time. When he was in prison, faced with a pending opportunity to testify before Caesar and possibly torture and death as well, he told the Philippians that he was confident he would not be ashamed. It wasn't self-confidence. He was depending on their prayers and on the continual supply of the Spirit. You can read the letter and hear how the Spirit was giving him joy in the Lord and deep peace in the face of uncertainty—as well as great love for his fellow believers. He loved them so profoundly that their need for him was just as important to him as his own desire to be with the Lord.

We especially need the Spirit to empower us to love. We need him to meet us at that powerless point where our self-centeredness meets his command, "Love one another. As I have loved you, so you must love one another." Jesus never, ever thinks selfishly; he gives himself to us all the time. He is completely engaged with us in love. How can we love that way? That shift of focus away from ourselves to a concern for others is a Copernican revolution, and all the laws in the universe can't bring it about. We certainly can't bring it about in ourselves. Only the Spirit can do it.

After Janet and I listened to Gordon teaching on Galatians, the two of us had a very significant prayer meeting. We were tired of wrangling over who was right and who was wrong and advocating for our own interests. Paul writes about union with Christ like it's the new exodus. He says that through Jesus' death we have died "to what bound us" and through his life we can "serve in the new way of the Spirit." We wanted that exodus; we wanted to live in that freedom.

We went to the Lord and told him we were sorry for the conflict that keep cropping up in our marriage and asked him to take our love for each other and make it deeper—to make it a love that was *kata pneuma*. There was no sound of rushing wind, no flaming tongues of fire, but there was a gentle humbling that came into our relationship. We've come to accept our continual need for this gospel-produced humbling, this freedom to lay down our weapons, because it's usually pride that turns our conversations into conflicts. When we start to get into an argument we've found we can pray and ask the Lord to break the deadlock—and he does. Prayer can be like a really good brainstorming session. Our self-centered mentality is a very small box and we're trapped inside of it. It never occurs to us there might be another way of looking at things. Then the Spirit comes in with a totally fresh perspective and we experience the exodus all over again. He humbles us and teaches us to look at things from each other's point of view, to enter into each other's world and sympathize with each other's weaknesses and needs.

So it was with the tomatoes. This time it wasn't a conflict with Janet; it was a conflict with two very small children, and it could have been a very *kata sarka* moment—because I love my tomatoes. Not those pale, picked-while-they're-still-green, poor excuses for a tomato you get in the produce department. I love tomatoes right off the vine, still warm from the sun, full of the taste of summer.

Every year I try to figure out how to grow tomatoes and have them ready to pick at the end of August. The trouble is, Janet and I go north every June. We drive away from the California sun where the tomatoes are thriving and head up the coast to Washington to spend a few months close to the Canadian office of our ministry. For us, the weather is lovely, but we've found that tomatoes don't much like cool and cloudy with a chance of rain.

One year I came up with a brilliant plan. I bought a few plants in California, where you can get them already covered with little green tomatoes, and drove them north. I was happily cruising along with my plants in the back when I saw those dreaded flashing red lights in my rearview mirror. I wasn't speeding. I'd learned the hard way not to do that in Washington, especially with a California license plate. I said to Janet, "I wonder if he spotted the tomato plants. Maybe he thinks they're marijuana plants." Sure enough. He asked me to roll down my back window, took a long look at our plants, and then said, "Okay, now I see the tomatoes. You can go."

On we went. The day after we arrived, my tomato plants were happily situated in perfectly improved soil in the sunniest spot we could find. We watered and fed and watched over them for three months. Janet even contrived a little tent for when there was too much rain so they wouldn't get sick. When the last week in August came all three plants had at least a few ripe red tomatoes on them. We'd sampled a couple already and they were the best I've ever tasted.

Then the two small children arrived. Janet and I were trying to have a conversation with their parents. The kids were bored so our friend Adrian, who was visiting for the week, kindly volunteered to take them out to the backyard. He played games with them and told them stories but eventually he needed a bathroom break. He was only gone for a few minutes but when he got back those two small children had picked just about every one of my tomatoes and smashed them on the ground or against the fence. Adrian was aghast. "What have you done? This is bad! You've destroyed all of Mr. Morris's tomatoes!"

The oldest, a little boy, looked around at the devastation and said, "Would you help us hide them?"

"No," said Adrian, "you can't hide them, that won't make it okay."

"Well . . ." The little boy thought for a minute. "Would you hide *us*?"

Let me freeze-frame the story for a minute just to give you time to notice what a perfect reenactment of the Garden of Eden this was.

Adrian found Janet in the kitchen and whispered, "The kids smashed most of Charles's tomatoes when I was in the bathroom." Janet and Adrian not only felt bad for me, they were both worried that I was going to get very, very angry.

The miracle was that I didn't. In fact, I laughed. But this isn't a story where I'm the hero; it's a story where Jesus is the hero. His Spirit was filling me with the joy of the Lord and it was relaxing my grip on my tomatoes. He was miraculously giving me compassion. Some people are hard to love—but Jesus breaks the deadlock by allowing us to see them with his eyes. Later I prayed for those little ones to know the One who came into the Garden and saw the devastation I wreaked on his creation and chose to send his Son to die for me.

Seeing how Jesus has loved us teaches us how to love other people. Only it's more mysterious than that and more powerful because it's the work of the Spirit. He fills our hearts with the love of Christ and it changes us into lovers. The commandments etched in stone never changed God's people but now he's etched them on our hearts through the gospel. How has Jesus loved us? When we try to count the ways we realize there's no end to them. The Spirit empowers our hearts to see this love, to be filled with it, and then to translate it into love for others. He evangelizes our hearts with the overwhelming love of Jesus so we can internally understand how to love other people.

You can see Paul employing this principle in his letter to the Galatians. He knows they're not a community of perfect people and he realizes their ability to love each other is going to be continually challenged. He knows that if they revert to trying to keep the law they'll start competing with each other and lose any sympathy they might have had for each other's weaknesses.

He also knows that the gospel produces an entirely different mindset. So he tells them, "Brothers and sisters, if someone is caught in a sin, you who live by the Spirit should restore that person gently. . . . Carry each other's burdens, and in this way you will fulfill the law of Christ."

"The law of Christ" is all the ways Jesus has loved us. We learn to love by feasting at the banquet of love Christ has spread out for us to enjoy and then offering it to others. How has he carried our burdens? We need to take time to savor this, to feel the burden lifted, to experience the relief, to fill up on his compassion for our weakness. We need to meditate on how gently he restores us when we sin; we need to sample his grace and tenderness. And then we can start to make his love our rule of life. That's how we walk in the Spirit. That's how the children of God are meant to live.

Spirit-people are gospel-transformed people. Paul tells the Galatians to "keep in step with the Spirit." The Spirit is our partner, and we're meant to follow his lead as we keep in step with the music of the gospel.

Paul told the Corinthians, "I am in the law of Christ." Christ's laid-down life of love had become the apostle's rule of life. It was shaping the way he lived. He was willing to become "all things to all people in order to save some" because he knew the Son of God had done that for him. He didn't just know it; he was encompassed by it, shaped by it, called by it. He laid down his own identity so he could freely identify with all kinds of people and he did it because Christ had identified with him. That's the kind of thinking we're meant to be doing—we're meant to connect the dots between how we've been loved and how we're called to love. The only thing that counts, Paul says, is "faith expressing itself in love" (Gal. 5:6 NLT).

The Macedonians are another example of how this works. Paul encouraged them to take up an offering for the poor in Jerusalem and he says they "exceeded his expectations" because "they gave themselves first of all to the Lord." They didn't just dig in their pockets; they gave their very lives to Jesus and then "gave as much as they were able and even beyond their ability."

Why did they do this? Because they were full of the gospel. They knew the truth that, "though he was rich, yet for your sake he became poor, so that you through his poverty might become rich." They didn't just know it; they marveled at it; they let it sink into their hearts until they knew how rich they really were. They understood that they had been united to Jesus in his life of love and that giving themselves to him meant giving themselves to others.

Of course the most heart-rending example happened in the upper room when Jesus humbled himself and washed our feet and then put his robe back on and sat down and looked us straight in the heart and said, "Now love one another as I have loved you."

We need to think about the massive love of Jesus so we'll see what a massive response it calls for in return. Then we'll be sailing with the wind because that's exactly the direction the Spirit wants to take us. The gospel is meant to create a Copernican revolution of love in God's people. Paul describes this in his letter to the Philippians. He says,

> Therefore, if you have any encouragement from being united with Christ, if any comfort from his love, if any common sharing in the Spirit, if any tenderness and compassion, then make my joy complete by being like-minded, having the same love, being one in spirit and of one mind. Do nothing out of selfish ambition or vain conceit. Rather, in humility value others above yourselves, not looking to your own interests but each of you to the interests of the others.

He sums it all up by telling them to "have the same mindset as Christ Jesus."

What a tremendous encouragement it is to be united to Christ. What a profound comfort it is to be loved by him. What a wondrous thing it is to know that we share the Spirit together and that he's pouring the tenderness and compassion of Jesus into our hearts. Paul is telling us to connect the dots. "In humility value others above yourselves," because that's what Jesus did for you. That's our daily calling—to take in the gospel and then live it out as the sons of God—to comprehend the mindset of Christ and then adopt that same mindset, that tender compassionate, self-giving mindset of Jesus.

The gospel isn't meant to just be a key that gets us into the house and then gets tossed aside—the gospel *is* the house. It's where we're meant to live. We need to keep on hearing this story because it contains the power of God to change our hearts—which is why Paul tells it to the Philippians all over again:

> In your relationships with one another, have the same mindset as Christ Jesus:
>
> Who, being in very nature God, did not consider equality with God something to be used to his own advantage;
>
> Rather, he made himself nothing by taking the very nature of a servant, being made in human likeness.
>
> And being found in appearance as a man, he humbled himself by becoming obedient to death—even death on a cross!

Part 3

MAKING HIS GLORY KNOWN

8

The
Reconciling Things

I (Charles) was convinced we should go to the stained glass Center City church with the full stop organ and choir. Moving from a small town in Oklahoma to the East Coast metropolis of Philadelphia meant making all new connections—new home, new doctors, new schools, and, of course, new church. As far as I was concerned, we belonged at the church with its deep historical roots and its solid reputation for biblical preaching. I was that kind of people. I knew a Brooks Brothers blazer when I saw one; I knew pure doctrine when I heard it, and I knew enough to appreciate the rich and solemn beauty of the ancient hymns they sang.

Janet had other ideas. There was this other church near our home that met in a gym. There were a few blue blazers scattered amongst the jeans of the leftover hippie-types and the medical scrubs of tired-looking people who seemed to have come straight to church after a rotation at the hospital. There was a band that burst into praise and a front row of men confined to wheelchairs who were swaying to the music. The first Sunday we visited, a man in a pin-striped suit casually slipped out his harmonica and started playing along. Seated a few rows over was a woman whose hat definitely belonged at a garden party sitting next to a man I was pretty sure belonged to a motorcycle gang. When the preacher stood up in the pulpit he beamed out at the congregation with a barely suppressed joy and said, "Greetings. My name is Jack Miller and I am a recovering Pharisee" and then, chuckling, he added, "and you're one, too, but don't worry—Jesus is a great Savior."

It was among this motley group of believers that I finally began to understand the kind of community the gospel creates.

Janet loved it. She went to work convincing me that this church was the better choice if for no other reason than that it was so much closer to our new home. After several Sundays of not getting ready in time to drive all the way to Center City, I agreed.

It took me a while to get comfortable with this uninhibited style of worship but eventually I did—and I even learned to love it. I want to give a disclaimer right up front and say that I'm not endorsing or criticizing any particular form of worship. We've worshiped in Anglican churches where the ancient beauty of the liturgy gets more profound as you repeat it week after week. At a Teen Challenge chapel we rejoiced with former drug addicts as they jumped up and down singing "I'm alive, I'm alive!" We've seen the beauty of our Malawian brothers and sisters dancing in the aisles like David dancing before the Ark of the Covenant. We've sung psalms in churches with no instruments where the simple beauty of our blended voices rose up in harmony to God. All over the world God's people are bringing him praise in beautiful ways. The truth never changes but the Spirit seems to produce an unlimited number of variations on the theme—and we can enjoy them all.

I also want to say that there was absolutely nothing wrong with that other church. To this day it is a lighthouse of gospel preaching. For years they've been reaching out to the center city world around them with the love of Jesus. But it was amongst this motley group of believers at the gym church that I finally began to understand the kind of community the gospel creates.

There was no danger of forgetting the gospel in this church or of turning it into some sterile doctrinal formulation. It wasn't something they pulled out and dusted off when they needed to share it with unbelievers. It was front and center all the time because the leadership of this church understood that Christians need to keep on being evangelized. We need to keep on hearing the gospel because the gospel contains the life-changing power of God and we tend to have gospel amnesia. We forget. We need to be reminded of Jesus—of who he is and what he's done—all the time. The more we hear it and take it in and realize what it means for us, the more we're changed, not just individually but as a people—as the people of God.

Jack Miller believed the one thing that cuts us off from grace quicker than anything else is our tendency to become like the Pharisees. We learned to be *recovering* Pharisees in the years we spent at this church, to see our propensity to lapse into self-righteousness and to keep on repenting for it. When Martin Luther nailed his ninety-five theses to the door of the church in Wittenberg the need for ongoing repentance was number one on his list.

We weren't the only ones who learned this lesson. When Mart and his wife moved to town they went church shopping just like we did. He was looking for a church whose worship conformed to the standards God had laid down in his Word. When he walked in the door of the gym he was pretty sure this wasn't it. When the worship leader invited anyone to stand up and pray, Mart started mentally crossing the gym church off his list. Then right next to him a woman rose from her seat with tears streaming down her face and said, "Thank you,

Jesus, for rescuing me from the life I was living, from the shame of selling my body. Thank you for loving me and saving me."

Mart was stunned. Her prayer deeply convicted him that in spite of all his doctrinal rightness he was getting it altogether wrong. Here she was pouring out her heart in gospel-produced worship while his heart was cold and critical. He realized that she was worshiping Jesus like the sinful woman in Luke 7 while he was not really worshiping him at all. He was more like Simon the Pharisee.

Simon had invited Jesus to dinner at his house after hearing him teach. While they were eating, a woman of the town "who had lived a sinful life" came in with an alabaster jar of perfume. Jesus was "reclining at the table" the way people did in that culture, so his feet were behind him. Luke says the woman went and stood behind Jesus with tears streaming down her face. When her tears started falling on his feet she undid her hair and bent down to dry them. Then she opened the alabaster jar and anointed them with perfume.

Simon was the polar opposite of this woman on every count. He was an upstanding religious leader with a sterling reputation. He didn't even extend Jesus the common courtesy of having his servants wash his feet as he normally would for a guest in his home. Why he had invited Jesus to dinner in the first place isn't exactly clear but he probably wanted to check him out to decide if he was truly a prophet or not. As for the woman, if she had dared to come near Simon he would have recoiled to avoid being contaminated by her sin. Religious purity was very important to the Pharisees, and Simon had already raised an eyebrow when Jesus failed to ritually wash his hands before the meal.

The fact that Jesus allowed the woman to touch him so freely convinced Simon that he wasn't a prophet after all. He clearly had no special prophetic insight or he would have known what kind of woman she was. He didn't say it out loud but he thought it, and Jesus corrected his thinking as only Jesus can do. He let him know that he had very special insight indeed—in fact he could read Simon's thoughts and he directly addressed those thoughts by telling a story about two men who both owed debts to a moneylender—one a very small debt and one a very large debt. The lender forgave both debts—he just wiped them off the books—and Jesus asked Simon, "Which of them will love him more?" Simon gave the obvious answer, "I suppose the one who had the bigger debt forgiven." Jesus went on to explain that the reason the woman loved him so much was that she knew the size of her debt.

There are two very shocking things about this story.

First, Jesus makes it very clear that loving him is the thing that matters. *Do you love me?* That's the issue on the table. Simon had other issues. He wanted to know if Jesus was a prophet. Jesus gave him indisputable evidence that he was but then he made it clear that he was much more than a prophet. The moneylender in the story is like God; he holds the debts of the other two men; he has the power to forgive their debt—and Jesus identified himself with the moneylender. He's the one with the power to forgive sins. Prophets don't talk that way; God talks that way. God is the one we're supposed to love with all our heart, soul, mind, and strength and Jesus was very clearly putting himself in the place of God.

Was it wasteful to do such an extravagant thing? Not when you consider the extravagant thing Jesus was going to do for her.

The second shocking thing was how he answers the question: *Who is going to love me more?* Actually, he makes Simon answer it. Who is going to love me more, Simon? Answer: the one who's been forgiven a very big debt. The one who's cast all his self-righteousness away and taken his place with the great big sinners. He's the one who loves Jesus with a great big cast-caution-to-the-wind worshiping kind of love.

That's who Jesus is looking for. He doesn't have a lot of interest in people who think they have little debts. He's looking for big debtors who understand that he's a big Savior who's paid a big price for their sin. "You see this woman, Simon?" Jesus asks, in effect "You should be like her."

The sinful woman in this story is a picture of just how liberating the gospel can be. She wouldn't have dared come under the condemning eye of that crowd, she wouldn't have dared to touch Jesus, the holiest of holies, if she hadn't known and believed that she was forgiven. Jesus loves her boldness. He loves her freedom. He loves it that she doesn't pay any attention to the judges in the room—that she has no doubt that her debt has been taken away—and that she only has eyes for him. And he loves it that she pours out her love for him. The jar of perfume she broke had a high price tag and she just recklessly poured it on his feet and filled the room with the sweetness of her love.

Was it wasteful to do such an extravagant thing? Not when you consider the extravagant thing Jesus was going to do for her. Her gift was nothing compared to the body of Jesus that was going to be broken and poured out for her—and for us. Nothing is more precious than the blood of the Son of God. Was it too extravagant a gift for him to make? He didn't think so. The Father didn't think so. Jesus poured himself out like sweet perfume as an atoning sacrifice for our sins. It was a sweet perfume to God the Father and it's a sweet perfume to us. And it's sweet perfume to him when we pour out our love in return.

To stay in that place we need to be continually offloading our own righteousness so our hearts can stay full of the gospel. That's what the leadership of this church understood and lived out and constantly promoted—that although Jesus wants us to be like the sinful woman we have a tendency to become like Simon. That's what we and Mart and a lot of other people came to understand at this church. We learned to recognize the "yeast of the Pharisees" in ourselves. Pharisees think they're always right. They have 20/20 vision when it comes to other people's sins and a congenital blindness to their own. They are self-appointed correctors. They have a strong sense of their own importance. They feel qualified to render judgments. They are completely unaware of how polluted they are inside. They're hypocrites, as Jesus so pointedly said, and they don't even realize it. And worst of all—they completely miss Jesus.

We need to be *recovering* Pharisees. We need to humble ourselves before the cross and let it strip us of our self-righteousness so we can worship Jesus with all of our hearts. We need the cross to do its humbling work in us again and again so we won't be putting up barriers to our fellowship with one another. When I walked into the gym church that first Sunday, I didn't realize how much of my own righteousness I was bringing in the door. I didn't see that I was creating a barrier between myself and this motley crew of people. But I learned. I came to understand why Paul was so upset when Peter refused to eat with the Gentile believers in Antioch.

Peter was freely eating with them without any qualms until a group of Jewish believers arrived and criticized him for not maintaining his distance. Then he stopped doing it; he moved to another table. Peter knew better. He knew that he was not only free to eat non-kosher food but also free to associate with Gentiles. The Lord taught him this lesson very specifically when he protested about going to the Gentile Cornelius's house to share the gospel. Jesus gave him a vision of all kinds of unclean animals and told him to eat them and stop calling unclean what God had made clean. So Peter went and preached the gospel to Cornelius, and he and his friends believed it and were filled with the Holy Spirit.

When Peter went back to report what had happened to the council in Jerusalem he made sure they understood the implications.

Brothers, you know that some time ago God made a choice among you that the Gentiles might hear from my lips the message of the gospel and believe. God, who knows the heart, showed that he accepted them by giving the Holy Spirit to them, just as he did to us. He did not discriminate between us and them, for he purified their hearts by faith.

Peter knew God had removed the distinction between Jew and Gentile, but apparently in Antioch he let peer pressure get the better of him. When Paul saw that he was withdrawing from his Gentile brothers and sisters he was ready to tear his hair out. Paul says he had to call Peter out in front of everyone because he was "not acting in line with the truth of the gospel." It's the same for us. When we draw a line and put ourselves on one side and other believers on the other side we're doing the same thing. We're not acting in line with the truth of the gospel.

The gospel has created a people with no distinctions. No barriers. No differences. It's touching to see how passionately Paul embraced this humbling truth. In the first three chapters of Romans he puts everyone in the same category, both Jews and Gentiles, by showing that we're all sinners, "There is no distinction; for all have sinned and fall short of the glory of God" (3:22–23 NASB). He puts himself squarely in that sinner category. In fact he knows that he's the chief of sinners.

All of us are on the sinner side of the line, but Paul doesn't stop there. He goes on to say that there's no distinction because "all are justified freely by his grace through the redemption that came by Christ Jesus." (v. 24) We've all been declared righteous in the sight of God on the exact same basis. Jesus has redeemed us all, he's taken us all out of condemnation into life. We've all experienced the same glorious exodus on the same level and on the same terms—the death and resurrection of Jesus. As he says a little later, "There is no distinction between Jew and Greek; for the same Lord is Lord of all, abounding in riches for all who call on Him" (10:12 NASB).

At the end of chapter 3 after Paul gets through explaining the need for the cross and he asks a rhetorical question, "Where, then, is boasting?" then he answers it: "It is excluded." When Paul says "boasting," he means making ourselves out to be someone special. That's what Peter's action at Antioch implied—we Jews are something special, we're better than you Gentiles. But when you understand the cross, when you see that Jesus had to die in order for you to be justified, where is the boasting? It is excluded. There is no difference.

> *We live in a world where we feel compelled to create identities for ourselves.*

We're all on the same side of the line, fully sinners, fully justified, fully blessed in Christ. But to get into that blessed place we have to check our boasting at the door.

The gospel is meant to be our defining reality. It's not just a key to get us in the door; it shapes how we think about ourselves and our brothers and sisters in Christ. The gospel doesn't just produce new individuals—it creates a new people. The Lord wants us to understand the implications of the gospel and to live them out in our lives together. He means for his death and resurrection to create a communion of deeply humbled people who know themselves to be both equally sinful and equally blessed—a people with no lines.

"For you are all sons of God through faith in Christ Jesus. For all of you who were baptized into Christ have clothed yourselves with Christ. There is neither Jew nor Greek, there is neither slave nor free man, there is neither male nor female; for you are all one in Christ Jesus" (Gal. 3:26–28 NASB).

We learned at the gym church that our identity as Christians is entirely grounded in Jesus. He is who we are. The gospel deconstructs our self-created identities, strips us of any sense of superiority we might be harboring, and then reconstructs us in Jesus. We have an entirely new identity that we share together in him.

We live in a world where we feel compelled to create identities for ourselves. For me going to the Center City church would have done that; it would have confirmed my self-concept. This is who I am. I am this kind of people. Our friend Mart had formed his identity around his theological correctness. We try to create ourselves through the organizations we belong to, the clothes we wear, our credentials and accomplishments, even our consumer choices.

A few months back a friend of ours posted on Facebook that her cellphone was irreparably broken and asked for suggestions on what to buy next. Of course she got lots of instant advice. One woman said, "Get an iPhone, dear, they're small and elegant and brilliantly intuitive. I wouldn't have anything else." Then a guy weighed in, "Apple is a big conspiracy. I wouldn't have an iPhone or an Apple computer either. I have a Dell, it's big and blocky like me but it's never failed to get the job done."

It was all tongue in cheek—but it was also revealing. There was some sort of identify formation going on that was connected to people's technological choices. We can see ourselves as the cool Apple type or as the anti-cool Dell type. We can base our identity on being in the Philadelphia Blue Book or being a blue-collar South Philly guy who thinks snobs are a joke. We can feel cool because we attend the classy Center City church or because we go to the down-to-earth church in the gym. Of course there are identities that go much deeper —our political affiliations and causes, our ethnicities and nationalities, our denominations and church memberships—but the important thing to understand is that all of our self-based identities are potentially divisive. They have a great tendency to become our boast, to feed our egos. They all draw lines. They all create divides.

John says the world is actually based on this system of boasting.

But we've been called out of the world into the kingdom of God through the cross of Jesus, and this calling of God requires us to leave our boasting at the door and to be completely identified with Jesus— and with one another. That's why the church is so wondrously diverse. That's why we can meet up with Christians from the opposite side of the globe and have such a deep common bond. That's why former prostitutes and recovering Pharisees can love each other and worship together with one heart—because Jesus is our common identity. He is who we are. We are all sons of God through faith in him: "Here there is no Gentile or Jew, circumcised or uncircumcised, barbarian, Scythian, slave or free, but Christ is all, and is in all" (Colossians 3:11).

She was prepared for primitive living conditions, but she wasn't ready for her fellow missionary.

Jesus said this oneness in his church would be a witness to the world. Just before he went to the cross he prayed and asked his Father,

> that all of them may be one, Father, just as you are in me and I am in you. May they also be in us so that the world may believe that you have sent me . . . I in them and you in me—so that they may be brought to complete unity. Then the world will know that you sent me and have loved them even as you have loved me.

Janet and I know from personal experience how easy it is to hear this and nod our heads in agreement—and yet how hard it can be to live it out in the body of Christ. We can so quickly let minor affronts and petty irritations and unspoken criticisms and little jealousies creep into our hearts. We can forget that the one real issue is demonstrating to the world that Jesus has torn down the "dividing wall of hostility" through his death and brought his people into a unity of love. The gospel is meant to produce a people who keep on tearing down that dividing wall and keep on renewing their love for one another. And the world is meant to see this miracle and be convinced that Jesus has done what no one else could ever do.

The story was leading up to this very point all along. The Exodus was meant to demonstrate the power of Israel's God so all the nations could see that he could do what no other so-called god could do. Ten plagues and the parting of the Red Sea certainly accomplished that goal. The surrounding nations were very impressed by the power of Yahweh to deliver them out of slavery, but in the end they saw Israel becoming just like all the other nations. But now God has done a new thing through his Son, he's accomplished a new exodus for his people. We're meant to be a demonstration to the world of the power of the crucified Son of God to deliver his people. We're meant to show by our love for one another that Jesus has done what no one else could ever done.

Jack Miller had a story he used to tell to show how critically important this is. It's the story of Florence Allshorn, who arrived on the mission field in Uganda in 1920—a young unmarried English woman full of zeal to serve the Lord. She expected culture shock; she expected the climate to be a hard adjustment, she was prepared for primitive living conditions, but she wasn't ready for her fellow missionary. This woman barely welcomed her. Instead she made sure Florence understood that the house they shared would be divided down the middle and she was never to trespass over to her side or touch her things.

Florence was disappointed, but she got busy with her missionary work of teaching the young Ugandan women about Jesus and tried to ignore the situation. But she couldn't. She was plagued by bitter feelings toward this other missionary. Finally she sadly told her students she was leaving. One of them came to her afterwards in tears and said, "Everyone leaves us. You teach us that Jesus saves but we haven't seen him save *this* situation."

The situation that needed saving was the one that goes all the way back to the genesis of the family, to the deep divide between brothers, to the hostility of Cain. Nobody had ever been able to save that situation and as far as this young Ugandan woman could see, Jesus hadn't been able to save it either. Florence realized the reputation of the Lord was at stake, so she decided to stay and for an entire year read 1 Corinthians 13 every day, praying for a change of heart.

Eventually she was able to forget her own hurt and have some compassion for the other woman's loneliness. She wasn't sure how to break through the barrier so she just started doing little loving things like taking notice of what the other woman liked. She gave her a book she thought she might enjoy and chose special items from the market for her to eat. Eventually the woman's heart began to melt, and before it was over they had become true friends. Jesus had saved the situation.

Later Florence reflected,

Our modern world wants peace . . . the church can go on exhibiting to the world (that this is the) place where that very thing it looks for is happening, little cases here and there of profound and real peace, in the midst of universal strife, and confusion. . . . Is it of blazing importance to us that they see this? Do we know in truth and in deed what really are the reconciling things?[1]

Note

1. Florence Allshorn, *The Notebooks of Florence Allshorn* (London: SCM Press, 1957), 20.

9

The Eyes of Jesus

It was a very human moment. His feet were tired, his throat was parched, and his head was probably aching from dehydration. The disciples had left him beside the well while they went to Sychar to get some food and he was sheltering there in the shade. A lone woman walked out of the gate of the town and made her way to the well. When she got there Jesus said to her, "Will you give me a drink?"

This woman knew Jews didn't talk to Samaritans. She especially knew that a Jewish man could occupy the same space with a Samarian woman until kingdom come and never acknowledge her existence, much less speak to her. So she came back at him a little saucy: "You are a Jew and I am a Samaritan woman. How can you ask me for a drink?"

Now listen to the Bridegroom make his offer to his bride: "If you knew the gift of God and who it is that asks you for a drink, you would have asked him and he would have given you living water."

This very ordinary moment is actually an extraordinary fulfillment of a marriage theme that weaves its way all through the Word of God. Whenever a man comes to a well in the Old Testament and asks a woman to give him a drink, he almost always finds a bride.

Anyone who knows the Bible well is going to hear wedding bells when they read this story of Jesus and this woman at the well. John starts to weave this marriage theme into his gospel in the second chapter. Jesus is at a wedding in Cana where he turns the water into wine and tells his mother his "time" has not yet come. Then in the third chapter John the Baptist declares that, "The bride belongs to the bridegroom. The friend who attends the bridegroom waits and listens for him, and is full of joy when he hears the bridegroom's voice. That joy is mine, and it is now complete." And now here in the fourth chapter Jesus is at this well asking a woman to give him a drink. John wants us to see that this is a profound moment of fulfillment. Jacob, Isaac, and Moses all found their brides in a divine appointment at a well, and now the Lord is finding his bride by a well, the bride he's been seeking throughout the story. And it's not just this one woman—it's everyone who puts their faith in him.

This woman represents all of us. The Son of God has taken on our flesh and bones and lowered himself to such a point of weakness that he needs to ask us for a drink of water. But then he offers what only God can give—living water to satisfy our deepest thirst. That's his proposal; he's offering us himself. He knows we're dying of thirst even if we don't know it ourselves and he wants us to drink deeply. He's fully aware of what it's going to cost him; he knows that before the water can gush forth he's going to have to be struck down.

God wove that message into the story too. In the wilderness the people were thirsty and crying out for water. The Lord told Moses that he was going to stand on a rock and that Moses should strike the rock with his staff so the water could gush forth. Now, here he is, the Lord in the flesh, on his way to being struck so his bride can drink.

We're that bride, the one he loved so much he was willing to die. We can see how intentionally he pursues us by watching him crash through all the cultural boundaries to get to this Samaritan woman. We can see how he perseveres in his love for us by watching him come back at her again and again, never giving up even when she treats him with disrespect and skepticism. Here she is, an outcast, an often married disreputable woman—and yet he wants her. The one who loves her and knows her has come to claim her for himself.

She's like Hagar, Hagar who wasn't Sarah, who was forced out with her son into the desert and was about to watch him die of thirst. But the Lord came to her and provided a well of water, and she named him *El Roi*—"the God who sees me." This woman at the well names Jesus with that same name. She runs back into town full of amazement and announces that she's met someone "who told me everything I ever did." He sees me. I am not invisible. I am not nothing. He sees deep into my heart, he knows "everything I ever did," all my sin and all my pain, and yet he wants to marry me.

We are all former Hagars who have now become Sarahs. Bilquis Sheikh saw it the first time she opened the New Testament and read where Paul quoted Hosea in Romans 9:25, "I will call her 'my loved one' who is not my loved one." So many threads of the story are coming together right here at this well.

God promised to pour out water onto the parched land, and now this water is gushing forth. We see it overflowing in this woman. She drinks the living water and runs back to Sychar and tells everybody in town about this man who knows her better than she knows herself.

It was a weak witness, but it sounded forth in Sychar like a trumpet because Jesus is seeking his bride. We don't need to know what to say, we can just say what she said, "Come and see him for yourself." The entire village came out to see Jesus, and after spending a few days in his presence they told the woman, "We no longer believe just because of what you said; now we have heard for ourselves, and we know that this man really is the Savior of the world."

Jesus was not just claiming his bride at this well—he was claiming the entire world. Jacob came to this very place and bought this exact parcel of land for a hundred pieces of silver long before the Israelites possessed the Promised Land. He was staking a claim by faith that the Lord would keep his promise to his father Abraham and give his people this land as their inheritance. But Jesus was staking claim to an even bigger promise. He was claiming not only this woman as his own—and the town of Sychar—and Samaria—but ultimately the uttermost reaches of the earth because he knew the Father had given him a promise. He wasn't just claiming Canaan; he was claiming all the nations of the world because he knew that in Psalm 2:7–8 God had said to him, "You are my son; today I have become your father. Ask me, and I will make the nations your inheritance, the ends of the earth your possession."

God told Abraham to look north, south, east, and west and then swore that his offspring would inherit everything his eyes could see. Jesus tells his disciples to look, too. He points at the fields all white and ripe around him and says, "Open your eyes and look at the fields: They are ripe for harvest." He wants us to see what he sees—to cast our eyes in every direction and take in, not just those visible fields, not just the land of Canaan, but the entire world. Jesus is telling us to look at the world and realize that it belongs to him. He rejoiced at the well at Sychar because he knew it was just the beginning, that one by one he would make his offer of living water, and one by one people from every nation would believe in him and tell others until God's kingdom extended over the entire world.

Jesus can see the glory of the future. He can see the Father's will finally being done. Soon he'll set his face for Jerusalem to be handed over and put to death to bring it to pass. Every fiber of his being is intent on offering the sacrifice that will bring salvation to the world. He knows this is the will of his Father and it is his meat and drink to do it—and he clearly wants us to be engaged in it with him. He wants us to have his eyes, to see what he sees, to be filled with his passion. He wants us to understand that right now the story is reaching its fulfillment and we get to be part of it.

After he left Sychar, Jesus continued on that long, circuitous route that inevitably took him to the cross, and the resurrection, and the ascension and finally—to Pentecost—when the Holy Spirit came pouring down from the Bridegroom onto the bride and she ran out into the street shouting the good news. He poured out the Spirit during the very feast instituted by God so long ago to celebrate the firstfruits of the harvest and three thousand came to faith in Christ. They were the true firstfruits of the true harvest—the one God has had his eyes on all along.

All the threads of the story are coming together; they've all been pulled together and fulfilled in Jesus—and in his bride. He's betrothed us in love and he's calling us to share his passion for the world. He's drafted us into his mission—and the one thing that will keep us from answering that call is idolatry. It's true for us like it was true for God's people in the Old Testament. It was

We don't intend to get sucked into the idolatry of our culture, but it happens before we know it.

idolatry that kept Israel from fulfilling her calling. She entered the Promised Land to claim it for her God but instead she got slowly sucked into the idolatrous practices of her neighbors. We face the same danger. John ended his first letter with the admonition, "Dear children, keep yourselves from idols." It's the idols that steal our hearts away from Jesus and stall our passion. It's the idols that hold us back so we can't enter into the joy of Jesus' vision of the harvest.

I (Charles) have discovered that even ministry can become an idol. I can be pouring heart and soul into proclaiming the glory of Jesus and all the while be harboring idols in my heart. One of my idols is sitting at the front of the room. In the Christian world we're not supposed to have places of special honor. James nailed us with his warning not to save the honored seats for the rich and famous but we do. We put the who's who in the most important spots up front on the dais and one of my idols is not to be left in the back. James doesn't mince words about the dangers of this "earthly" mentality. He says straight up that friendship with the world is enmity toward God but we still make friends with the world.

We don't intend to get sucked into the idolatry of our culture, but it happens before we know it. We end up like Woody Allen in the movie *Manhattan*. His family was all gathered around the table for Passover, but their atheist neighbors were making so much noise it was interfering with their meal. Woody Allen's character stood up, put down his napkin, and headed over to tell them to have a little respect. A while later he came back with pork chop on his breath and announced to his family, "Religion is the opiate of the people."

Jesus said we can't serve two masters and yet I try to do it. What cures me is just to sit down with Jesus and let him talk to me about it. In Luke 14 Jesus was at a banquet at the home of a prominent Pharisee and he noticed how all the guests were picking the places of honor for themselves. He took that golden opportunity to explain that his kingdom isn't meant to operate that way. In his kingdom we're meant to humble ourselves and choose the lowest places for ourselves. Whenever I realize I'm yearning for the limelight or wanting that special notice other people seem to be getting I can just listen to Jesus' words and it humbles me every time. It makes me realize that it really is *his* limelight I'm vying for and truly, I don't want it. I want him to have the glory.

I struggle with coveting the preaching gifts of others. When I hear my friend Alistair Begg on the radio it almost always punches that covetous button in my soul. Why don't *I* have a Scottish accent, Lord? But what cures me is the realization that we aren't competing with each other in Christ's kingdom. That's the way the world operates but we don't have to be that way because it *all* belongs to us. All our brothers and sisters and all their gifts are part of our inheritance. The Lord has given each of us exactly the gifts he means for us to have, not so we'll go seeking applause for ourselves, but so we can build up the body of Christ. The Lord gives me the gifts I need to do what he's called me to do just like he does for each of us.

Idols have a very subtle but powerful influence on our hearts. On that mission trip to that South Asian neighborhood in London we realized that there really is spiritual power at work behind those seemingly innocuous little Hindu statues. We felt it ourselves. Idols hold people in fear, but the missionaries who stayed and planted a church in that neighborhood have seen one person after another walk out of that life of bondage. They can do it because Jesus disarmed the powers and principalities when he died on the cross. He set his people free to serve the living God and "if the Son sets you free, you will be free indeed." Our secular idols have the same kind of power but we can walk out too, just like those former Hindus do. We just need to realize we're free to do it.

Janet and I had a very liberating moment several years ago when we were driving home from a summer vacation. It was early Monday morning. The sermon the day before had been on Matthew 6 where Jesus says it's impossible to serve both God and money. The preacher kept saying, "Money is not your master anymore." As we drove home we realized how bound we really were to serving money. It's not that we wanted to be rich—although we, like so many, sometimes dream of the life money could buy us.

> *Money isn't just tied to our desires; it's tied to our fears.*

But money isn't just tied to our desires; it's tied to our fears. Idols work on us from both directions. Janet and I had been anxiously trying to pay down our debt and save a little for our old age, and it was keeping our noses to the grindstone. As the old song goes, "Saint Peter, don't you call me 'cause I can't go; I owe my soul to the company store." Jesus said the worries of life can choke out the seed of the kingdom, and we could see how true that was in our life. But the words of that sermon began to have a liberating effect as we realized we didn't owe our souls to money, we owed them to the Lord and we were free to give ourselves to him. We could start living the good life right then and there.

I (Janet) have had a recent struggle with the idol of art—which I'm convinced is up there with money, sex, and power as the leading potential idols in our culture, along with politics, looking good, succeeding, getting applause, finding true love, running marathons . . . the list goes on and on but the point is not to be enslaved by anything, not to be mastered, not to make anything the be all and end all of our life—except for Jesus and his glory.

I realized a couple of years ago that with the kids long grown there was room in my life to do something I'd wanted to do for a long time—paint. Charles is the family ear and I'm the family eye. He finds transcendent joy in music and I find it in the visual arts. So I started painting—with a passion. The trouble was, the more intense I got about painting the less intense I was about serving the Lord. Jesus said it's not just our anxieties that choke out the seed of the kingdom—our desires do it too. I realized my heart was being hijacked by this new passion—so I gave it all up and donated my art supplies to Goodwill. But then I returned the next week hoping they'd still be there so I could buy them back.

I couldn't understand it. God made us in his image; he gave us the gift of creativity, so why was this creative thing dousing my love for the Lord?

One morning reading Hosea I got my answer. For thirteen chapters God tells his people they've been like an unfaithful wife. Finally in chapter 14 he says, "Return to the Lord your God" and "take words with you." He even gives them the words to take: "Forgive all our sins and receive us graciously, that we may offer the fruit of our lips. . . . We will never again say 'our gods' to what our own hands have made."

As I read Hosea I knew that I'd been an unfaithful wife to the Lord, and it broke my heart. I went to him with words and said, "Forgive me, Lord. I've been grabbing this goodness for myself like Gollum. I've been treating the 'art world' as an arena for my own glory. I've been competing with people and coveting their success. I've been looking for approval from the artists I admire. I've been saying 'my god' to the work of my hands."

> *Every good thing in life has this dual potential. We can either hold it tight or we can give it to God.*

It was a wonderfully liberating repentance. Every repentance is a rescue; grace always comes like a father with his arms outstretched to meet us, and that's what happened to me. I was forgiven and my heart was captured again for Jesus. But I still needed some assurance that I could continue to live in this worshipful way. A few verses later the Lord gave me just what I needed. He promised to heal his people's waywardness and love them freely because his anger had turned away from them, and he ends with this great assurance: "Your fruitfulness comes from me."

That's what I needed to hear: that promise from God that sets us free from trying to change ourselves. I kept thinking I needed to be a Gideon and smash my idol like he smashed his father's statue of Baal. Finally I realized that Jesus is my Gideon. He will smash our idols. *He* will heal our waywardness; *he* will make us fruitful. *He* will constantly renew our love for him and set us free from serving other gods.

Last summer there was a tiny bird fluttering from atop the double-hooked pole that holds our feeder—fluttering but going nowhere. I went out to see what was wrong and realized his foot was caught in the joint between the two hooks. I pushed it up and away he flew. So our Lord promises to do for us. We just keep on repenting and he will keep on healing our waywardness. Whenever I feel stuck I can cry out to him for help and he sets me free—again and again. I can be "in" the art world without being "of" it. Passion for art can be channeled into passion for Jesus and for his kingdom and his glory.

Every good thing in life has this dual potential. We can either hold it tight or we can give it to him; we can worship it or we can worship him through it. It really is all a matter of love. Who do we love? Who has our heart?

Love is at the heart of it all. For our young friend Marci it all came down to one very simple question, a question Jesus was asking her to answer. We asked her to share her story:

For as long as I can remember I wanted to have children. As a little girl I even dreamed of being a teacher so that I could be surrounded by children on a daily basis—until I could have some of my own. I had no idea the grip this idolatry of family had on my heart. The Bible talks about children being a gift from God, and I always thought my motives were holy and pure. I longed day in and day out for God to give me the desires of my heart. The problem was that those desires were not surrendered to God and his authority to do his perfect will in my life. I wanted to be a mommy more than I wanted anything else in the world. The wonderful gift of motherhood had become my sole ambition in life. It was what I lived for, my deepest longing.

When my husband and I got married I knew that I wanted children right away. Little did I know we would have to wait seven years before the birth of our first daughter. Each day, each month, each year that passed increased my pain, anxiety and feelings of emptiness. I felt like something was missing in my life and in my marriage. I truly believed that children would fill all those empty places in my heart.

My ever-wise God needed to remind me that the only thing that will ever truly satisfy me is himself, and that anything I give my worship to is sin. He began the process of extracting that idol from my heart. I'll never forget the moment I truly surrendered it to him. I was reading my Bible and praying one morning. My heart was so broken over not being pregnant yet again. I cried out to the Lord in desperation for him to fulfill this insatiable longing. Then I heard the Holy Spirit prompting my heart with this question, "Marci, what if I never give you children? Would you still love me?" I was stopped in my tracks. "Lord, you know my heart," I said. The Spirit prompted again: "I want you to say it." It took me several tries, but little by little I felt idolatry being uprooted from my heart. I was on my knees, desperate to surrender my idol to Christ. Finally, through painful tears, I uttered the words, "Lord, if you never give me children I will still love you and I will still follow you." I have to admit that I felt a hole where that idol had been—but only temporarily. Christ overwhelmed me in that moment with his comforting presence and I knew that as long as he was with me I could go on. Over time the desires of my heart began to transform into the desires of his heart.

Idolatry really is a matter of the heart. Thomas Chalmers didn't have much of a heart for the Lord at all. He was a clergyman in the early 1800s in Scotland but he didn't see any reason to spend more than one day a week fulfilling his pastoral duties. We saw his portrait hanging in the gallery of former principals of the New College School of Divinity at the University of Edinburgh. A friend took us in to see it and told us how Chalmers was deeply committed to caring for the poor. Something had radically changed him from that languid young rector into a man energized by his concern for the needy.

We did some research and found out that at the age of twenty-nine he had fallen dangerously ill and had spent the long weeks of his recuperation reading the works of William Wilberforce.[1] Day after day he heard Wilberforce describe how his passion for Jesus fueled his passion to see the horrors of slavery brought to an end. Chalmers left his bed a new man. In his most famous sermon, "The Expulsive Power of a New Affection," he explained that the only thing with the power to expel our idolatrous loves is the love of Jesus. Jesus captures our hearts and then fills them with the desires of his own heart.

Last summer I (Janet) asked the Lord to give me those desires. I kept hearing God say in the Bible how much he cares about the poor and the suffering and I realized I didn't really care. After I finished praying, immediately after, I opened an email expecting to read one of the lovely devotional thoughts this woman usually writes. Instead I read an impassioned plea that included a link to a story about women being trafficked. I opened it and wept. I read the horror stories and I groaned with pain. I realized with awe that I was getting a breathtaking, intimate experience of the very heart of Jesus and that he really is El Roi—the God who sees. He is wrenched with compassion for the suffering of the world and he wants to include us in that wrenching, to draft us into his heart, to unite us with himself. When he was with the woman at the well he *felt* her thirst in his own parched throat. His heart breaks with love for both our physical and spiritual needs and he wants his bride not just to love him but to share his heart and to be compelled by his compassion.

Paul said, "Christ's love compels us." Again and again I (Charles) realize that I need this love of Christ. I keep finding myself in a lackluster state of indifference. I need to ask Jesus to fill me with the compelling power of his own love. We need him to call us into his life so we can share his passionate commitment to the world. We need him to give us his eyes to see the harvest so we can join his great enterprise and be engaged in this culminating stage of the story. We're his church, his bride, so we get to be part of what he's doing and even though it's wrenching at times it truly is the good life.

We *all* get to be part of this good life. We can each one ask the Lord to engage our hearts in the cause of his kingdom. There's a multiplicity of ways that we can be involved, both close to home and far away. We can enter into the pain of others the way he entered into ours. We can open our eyes to suffering and allow our hearts to break open into acts of compassion. We can participate in his great nation-gathering venture even if we haven't been called to the mission field. The Lord connected us to that neighborhood in London all those years ago and even though we haven't been back for years it is still our field, so we can take personal joy in what's happening there.

W. O. Fraser had a committee of women back in England supporting him as he brought the gospel to the Lisu people in China. He knew they were as much a part of God's love for this people as he was and that their prayers and financial support were just as crucial to what God was doing among them. He suggested that all of us in the church see ourselves as homesteaders looking for our parcel of land.[2] We can't all work the whole world but each of us can stake our claim for the kingdom and join with others in developing some particular part of the world.

Jesus is calling us to share his passion—because we're his bride. We're the fulfillment of the woman in Proverbs 31 who is worth far above rubies to her husband. She not only works hard to clothe her own family, she opens her arms to the needy and extends her hand to the poor and she "considers a field and buys it; out of her earnings she plants a vineyard." We're his bride and he's calling us to share his entrepreneurial spirit, to see what he sees—a world that is ripe for harvest.

Notes

1. Michael Reeves, *Delighting in the Trinity* (Westmont, Ill.: IVP Academic: 2012), 110–11.

2. Eileen Fraser Crossman, *Mountain Rain* (Littleton, Colo.: OMF International: 2001), 100.

10

The Dawn of an Expected Day

Our grief was raw, too raw to take up our lives again. The Lord had given us deeply consoling realizations of his love from the moment we got the call about our son's death, but we were still not ready to go back home to California. Not yet. Instead we headed south to Dallas, where we knew our friend Dan Duncan would be preaching God's Word the following day. Sunday morning we were there in church, listening to the call to worship with sad but expectant hearts.

Dan did a little double-take of surprise when he spotted us out in the congregation and then started preaching from Mark 9. His sermon was about the father who brought his demon-possessed boy to Jesus for healing. I (Charles) could completely identify with the pain that father must have felt after years of watching his son self-destruct. I could feel his desperation as he told Jesus about begging his disciples to heal his son and how they couldn't do it. But what about his overwhelming joy when Jesus gave him back his son, whole and healed? A friend told us later Dan felt bad when he saw me sitting in the pew, knowing he was going to be preaching that particular story. After all, Jesus hadn't given our son back. No intervention for us, no celebration, just a son we finally lost, end of story. Only it's not the end of the story because there's a great day rising up for those of us who believe in Jesus.

We know our grief is just a drop in the bucket when you consider the suffering of so many others. We have a friend who barely made it to the funeral of her infant grandson because the pain of her cancer was so intense. A month later she was gone. She sat at that funeral knowing the same genetic disorder that took this little grandson's life was threatening the life of another one of her grandsons. Two months later he was gone too at the age of seven. Other brave believers worldwide are imprisoned for sharing their faith, sentenced to death. How many others have endured as much or more for the sake of Jesus? If we were to pile together all the suffering of God's people the weight would overwhelm us—except for one fact: "Our present sufferings are not worth comparing with the glory that will be revealed in us." There's a glory up ahead and it's going to far outweigh all our present pain. Our suffering is not the end of the story.

For years we'd been focused on the prospect of seeing Jeff restored. We believed the Lord could do anything and we kept imagining what it would be like to see our son fully liberated and in his right mind. We'd prayed for it, we'd expected it to happen right here in the land of the living, so when he died we were left in a state of confusion. "Why, Lord? Why didn't you give us back our son like you did that man?" His response was simple. He didn't explain; he just let us know we needed to wait. He suffused our hearts with the hope of the glorious Day of the Lord and told us to wait for it because it's coming soon, in just a little while.

The LORD Almighty will prepare a feast of rich food for all peoples, a banquet of aged wine—the best of meats and the finest of wines. On this mountain he will destroy the shroud that enfolds all peoples, the sheet that covers all nations; he will swallow up death forever. The Sovereign LORD will wipe away the tears from all faces; he will remove his people's disgrace from all the earth. The LORD has spoken.

Those verses from Isaiah 25 gave us a much bigger hope for the future than just seeing our son again—although we trust we will. We can almost imagine the sweet moment when Jesus will say, "Behold your son" and there he'll be, our Jeff, completely restored to life. But it's not just seeing Jeff; it's seeing Jesus that will finally heal our hearts. To see his face, to have his hand wipe away every one of those tears we still weep, to be remade in him, to enter into his joy—that's our hope. And it's more than just our own personal hope; it's the hope of the entire world. It's more than knowing we'll go to heaven when we die; it's knowing the day of the Lord is coming when Jesus will remake the cosmos.

The day of the Lord has always been part of the ultimate hope of the story. There's always been a forward movement to God's unfolding drama, beginning with the promise in the garden that a seed of the woman would come and crush the head of the serpent. His people have always been waiting in hope for God to break into his world and bring redemption.

Both his promises and his warnings are woven all through the Bible like a building crescendo that finally burst forth in joyous fulfillment when Jesus was born. Isaiah 60:1 says the arrival of the Day of the Lord is like a great light dawning for God's people, "Arise, shine, for your light has come, and the glory of the Lord rises upon you." The day has dawned in Jesus—but there's still a future dawning up ahead—the final full dawning of the day of the Lord is still to come.

Practically every kingdom parable Jesus ever told had this future orientation in mind. He wants this day to be fixed in our souls. He announced that his kingdom had come right then and there, that it is a present reality. But at the same time he consistently pointed to a glorious future culmination for those who put their faith in him. Everything will be set to rights on that day. Wickedness will be punished and God's people will be vindicated, the earth will be purged of death and sorrow and remade in glory—and Jesus will finally be glorified in the presence of the entire world.

> *The future wedding feast is the best possible news for those of us who believe—but for those who don't, it's a warning.*

Peter tells us to wait for it, to be faithful and wait until "the day dawns and the morning star rises in [our] hearts." He wants to instill this glorious hope in those who trust in Jesus but at the same time he wants to give a warning to the mockers. There will be a great separation on that day with no middle ground. This same dual message surrounds every prophecy in the Bible about the day of the Lord—joy for those who believe, but for those who don't, a day of terror.

Jesus himself always included both joy and warning whenever he talked about his return. "The kingdom of heaven is like a king who prepared a wedding banquet for his son," he said. The Bible consistently represents that day as a joyous feast for God's people and in Revelation we discover it's actually a wedding feast—*our* wedding feast. Jesus had his heart fixed on that day from the moment he set off to win his bride. He's so exultant with love he's planning to make us sit down at the table so he can serve us. Our minds boggle at the prospect and when we suffer it just intensifies the yearning. He's not just going to serve us; he's going to make sure we're dressed for the occasion by adorning us with himself. The creation "waits in eager expectation for the children of God to be revealed." The sight of Jesus is going to transform our very selves. "We shall be like him, for we shall see him as he is."

The future wedding feast is the best possible news for those of us who believe—but for those who don't, it's a warning. Jesus actually told this parable of the father preparing a wedding feast for his son as a warning to the world not to be so busy about their own business that they ignore the Father's invitation. Don't miss out on this; this is what really matters.

Another time he warned his followers not to be like the bridesmaids who couldn't be bothered to replenish the oil in their lamps. He wants us to stay focused on the great day. He wants us to stay in love with him and not let our first love wane into some lukewarm affection that isn't worthy of his sacrifice. A passionate groom should be met by a passionate bride. Paul pronounced his anathema on anyone "who does not love the Lord," and the Bible ends with the Spirit and the Bride crying, "Come!" Our love for Jesus is meant to have us eagerly looking for our wedding day. Love fuels our hope and hope fuels our love and together they fuel our lives.

Paul concluded his long letter to the believers in Rome with a prayer that the transforming power of hope would fill them to the very brim, "Now may the God of hope fill you with all joy and peace in believing, that you may abound in hope by the power of the Holy Spirit." All the apostles tell us to live our lives in light of that day, to be focused and sober and full of joy because we know it's coming and it's coming soon. The time is short. Put it on your calendar.

When we saw the recent movie version of the musical *Les Misérables*, we came away amazed by how the character Jean Valjean embodies this life of hope we're meant to live. The story opens with his release from prison after years of hard labor. He walks away thinking he's left his misery behind, only to discover that the world isn't exactly welcoming him with open arms. No one will hire him; no one wants him around, but then at his moment of deepest despair a bishop of the church invites him into his home, sits him down at his dinner table, filthy as he is, and shares a meal with him like they're brothers.

Right away you start to see that the character of the bishop looks a lot like Jesus, but then the resemblance gets even stronger. Valjean is so conditioned to hatred and so hardened in his heart that he steals away in the night with the bishop's valuables stashed in his bag. In the next scene the police drag him back to the house, shove him to the floor, and announce they've caught him red-handed.

By now you've gotten used to everyone singing instead of talking. The bishop begins to sing a song of amazing grace, telling the police that he actually gave those things to Valjean and reminding Jean that he's forgotten to take the rest of his gift. Then he takes a pair of solid gold candlesticks and presents them to an astonished Jean. After the police are gone the bishop tells him that he has redeemed his life for God and Jean leaves a new man.

From then on, wherever he goes he takes the candlesticks with him and places them in a prominent place in his home. They're always there, like three days on his calendar. They remind him of that day when he was purchased by God's grace. As Paul says, "You have been bought with a price!" They remind him that today he's called to live out his redemption, to have his thoughts and actions shaped by the love he has received, even if it means more suffering. But they also remind him of the future. One day he's going to enter into the fullness of glory.

In the last scene Valjean sings his final prayer to God, "Forgive me all my trespasses and take me to your glory." We realize he's been living for this day all along. This hope has kept him alert to the ultimate ramifications of how he was living his life. This hope has given him the perseverance to carry on. As he leaves his present life behind you see him walking into the future where thousands of candlesticks are brightly burning and you know he's finally come home. Every step of his walk, every day of his life had been leading up to this glorious day of joyous fulfillment.

It's the same for us. We live in space and time, and time relentlessly marches on. The good things inevitably succumb to their bondage of decay and slip through our fingers. They recede as we move forward to the day of our own dissolution. But in Christ time is transformed. In Christ we get a new calendar. Yesterday transforms today and fills it with the glorious promise of tomorrow's coming day. Life takes on a feel of anticipation when we live it with this new calendar—it starts to get big. It wakes us up to the ultimate significance of what we're doing right here and now. We're meant to "let the future sanctify the present to highest uses,"[1] as Spurgeon puts it. It turns every good thing we enjoy today into a foretaste of the future that's sure to come. It turns every sad thing we suffer today into a promise that one day this will be removed—swallowed up and taken away—and replaced by the ultimate good the Lord has stored up for the coming age.

Peter says we've been reborn into "an inheritance that can never perish, spoil or fade" that's being "kept in heaven for you." He tells us to be "prepared to give an answer to everyone who asks you to give the reason for the hope that you have." Our hope is meant to create a noticeable difference in our lives, so noticeable that we might actually be asked to give an explanation for it.

I (Charles) will never forget the day I prayed on my way to the pharmacy for an opportunity to witness. I walked to the back to get my prescription and stood at the counter while the pharmacist finished it up. He explained that he was a little slow that day because it was his first day back at work after a serious illness.

"In fact," he told me, "I actually died. I'm not a religious man but my soul actually left my body and entered this bright light and you will never guess who I saw!"

"No," I said, hoping he was going to say Jesus. "I can't guess. Who did you see?"

151

"Elvis! I saw Elvis!"

It wasn't exactly the witnessing opportunity I was expecting. It made me realize how important it is not to offer our own personal experiences as a reason for hope. A lot of people have experiences. This man was convinced there was a great light in his future. He was holding on to a hope that had nothing whatsoever to do with Jesus. True hope isn't based on our own personal experiences; it's based on the great objective intervention of God into his world through his Son. True hope looks at a "definite reality in history and announces the future of that reality."[2] I pray that I was able to communicate the difference to this man. It's not our personal disembodied experiences that give us hope; it's the guarantee of an entirely new creation that began at the resurrection of Jesus. It's a future given to the world by God at the price of his own Son, a big all-encompassing hope that "suffuses everything here in the dawn of an expected day."[3]

Charles and I (Janet) have lived a sort of nomadic life. There've been thirteen moves to date and except for the few years in the Rocky Mountains we've almost always lived in a rental. I've longed for us to have our own place where I could plant a garden and have a picket fence and know that we're finally settled. A few years back I casually mentioned this to the Lord. A little later I was reading a poem by Robert Browning written when he was in some tropical place longing for home: "Oh, to be in England now that April's there" he writes, and then ends remembering "the buttercups, the little children's dower— Far brighter than this gaudy melon flower."

As I read it my heart was filled with a longing for home. I freely admit to being an Anglophile, so any description of rural England stokes these fires. It felt like the Lord, who knows me so well, was stoking them on purpose. Somehow reading the words of that poem confirmed in my heart that I *will* have that yearned-for home one day —maybe not here and now but certainly then—and that all the children will be seated around the table.

Buttercups are the little children's dower. Someday God's children are going to inherit the entire created cosmos. The Lord committed himself to his creation when Jesus took on flesh and blood and when he was raised he raised the good earth with him. This world we love is going to be remade with nothing lost of all its goodness. I can look at buttercups now, raising their golden heads, and know what they're saying: "Soon, very soon, the day is going to dawn." Hope opens up the meaning of things and the buttercups start to testify. We can dig in our garden or warm our hands over a fire or feel the rain on our faces and know we're living out our destiny as the heirs of creation.

We don't get to visit our grandkids often enough, so every visit has a tinge of bittersweetness to it. When our little Gracie comes bouncing in to join us for breakfast, exuberantly chattering away, it's as sweet as honey and yet it's a little sad too because we know a several month separation is looming. But at the same time we have this great consolation that one day there will be no more separations. Joy isn't slipping through our fingers; it's just giving us a foretaste of what's ahead—a promise of a coming day when there will be no more pain and no more sorrow.

The Lord uses our present sorrows to intensify our anticipation of that future joy. I (Charles) grew up wearing a metal brace on my polio-affected leg. At first I didn't realize I was different but eventually the message got through. It was crushing when another child would point and whisper, "Mommy, what's that thing on his leg?" In my teens I had corrective surgery almost every summer to help me walk. It's one of those reminders that life here is not what it's meant to be.

Every time I read the word *lame* in the Bible it's always pointing forward to a great healing when the lame will leap with joy. The bodies we have now are not the end of the story. We have a great hope, a great coming day, and right here in the midst of our pain the dawn of that expected day is shining its joyous light. I have the promise that my body is going to be remade as part of the great remaking of the cosmos.

Our daughter Kate was just recently reminiscing about the great sorrow that came into her life when they adopted our grandson Ricky from Korea. Kate's brother had just died, and she was grieving for him and feeling a little panicked about only having one brother left. It seemed like a good thing to adopt a child so Grace and Charlotte would have another sibling. It was also an altruistic thing to do, a particularly Christian thing to do, so they started the long, expensive process.

> *The slag will be gone, the polio will be gone, the autism will be gone, and the world will be filled with joy.*

It never occurred to Kate it might be hard to love an adopted child, but from the day Ricky arrived at four months of age he was hard to love. He screamed all the time and demanded constant attention. It only got worse as he got older and it became clear that something was very wrong. He didn't talk; he didn't play normally. At the age of three he started pounding his legs, banging his head, and screaming almost incessantly. Nothing could console him. Up until then the doctors had been reluctant to give a diagnosis but finally after an exhaustive pediatric evaluation they said that Ricky was autistic, severely mentally retarded, and would never make significant progress.

Kate took the bull by the horns and poured herself into a three year, forty hour a week, life-consuming program of therapy. Now, at the age of nine we know Ricky isn't mentally retarded. He's autistic but he's happy much of the time and rarely intentionally hurts himself. He's able to talk a little and express affection, and best of all—he loves the Lord. Kate says the turning point for her was realizing she couldn't control the situation but that the Lord was with her in it. Once she relaxed she developed a deep, protective love for her little boy. She knows the Lord will completely transform him when he comes again but until then Ricky is going to need his parents. Our son-in-law, Rich, had always planned for them each to have a motorcycle after the kids were grown but now he says they're going to need a sidecar for Ricky. Still, the rest of their lives is only the short run—they know the long run holds a complete healing for their son.

Richard Llewellyn's novel *How Green Was My Valley* tells the story of a coal mine in Wales that provided income for the locals and fuel for thousands of furnaces and stoves. The downside was that it slowly filled the valley with slag. The book is a lament over the loss of beauty, but it ends with the day of the Lord breaking through and restoring the freshness and verdant beauty of the earth. One day the world will be subsumed by a healing glory and all the things we love will still be there. The slag will be gone, the polio will be gone, the autism will be gone, and the world will be filled with joy—all sweet and no bitter.

Even now we can taste it. When we sit down with believing friends to enjoy a meal and savor our mutual love for Jesus we're getting a taste of the future joy. When we worship together as believers and fill up on the beauty of the Lord it's a preview of the coming attraction—and sometimes it's almost too much to handle.

When we took that two-week course with Darrell Johnson on the book of John, the beauty of Jesus was almost too much for us to bear. On the last day of class Darrell zeroed in on the final few hours of Jesus' life and took us very slowly through it, step by step. We saw the beauty of Jesus displayed before our very eyes like we'd never seen it before. We heard his ineffable words of love when he intentionally handed himself over to death for our sakes: "If you are looking for me, then let these men go." His glory flashed out for just a second, just enough to make his arresting mob fall to the ground and to demonstrate for all the ages that he could have brought it all to a halt with his little finger.

But he didn't. He sheathed his glory and let them take him away. We followed his majestic progress through the hatred of the trial and Pilate's indifference and the cruelty of the soldiers. We watched all the way to the cross, up to the moment when he cried out, "It is finished" and breathed his last. By the end there were tears streaming down all of our faces. The beauty was so intense it hurt. Later some friends asked us how we enjoyed the class and we just shook our heads and said, "It was death by Jesus."

Jeremy Begbie says if we're looking for beauty we should look right there, to that story. The greatest beauty in all creation is found "in a trinity of inexhaustible love and life, active and present in the world . . . and never more intensely than in the saving life, death and resurrection of Jesus Christ."[4] That very beauty is going to fill the new heavens and the new earth. The New Jerusalem will have the gold of that story woven all through it. We're going to be there together, bonded by the sight of his beauty, and "voicing creation's praise"[5] for all we're worth.

Notes

1. Charles Spurgeon, *Morning and Evening* (Peabody, Mass.: Hendrickson Publishers: 2002), 552.

2. Jurgen Moltmnn, *Theology of Hope* (Minneapolis: First Fortress Press: 1993), 16

3. Ibid., 17.

4. Jeremy Begbie, *The Beauty of God* (Westmont, Ill.: IVP Academic: 2007), 21.

5. Jeremy Begbie, *Voicing Creation's Praise* (Eugene, Ore.: Wipf and Stock Publishers: 2003).

11

How Not to Miss Jesus

They're lost in the dark world of their own erroneous thoughts, those two disciples, as they put one heavy foot in front of the other, trudging back to Emmaus. It was bewildering. Just days before they'd been hurrying in the opposite direction filled with hope that this Passover it would finally happen—Jesus would finally declare himself to be the Messiah. The whole city had been alive with expectation. Crowds had danced and shouted Hosanna as Jesus made his majestic, gentle entrance into Jerusalem on the colt of a donkey. They'd been riding high that day but now, just three days later, they're reeling from the shock of his public humiliation and his horribly gory death.

As they walk along, talking it all over, shaking their heads, a stranger comes up alongside them, obviously wanting to get in on their conversation.

"What are you discussing together as you walk along?" he asks and they stand stock still in surprise.

"Are you the only one visiting Jerusalem who does not know the things that have happened there in these days?"

"What things?" the stranger asks as if he's completely unaware of anything out of the ordinary. They pour out the whole story, how Jesus of Nazareth was a prophet, powerful in his words and deeds, how God and all the people of Israel saw it but, incredibly, the chief priests and rulers delivered him up to be condemned to death. And then in a sad clincher they tell him, "We had hoped that he was the one who was going to redeem Israel." To make matters even more confusing, Jesus' body has gone missing and some of their women are insisting that he's alive, that they have it on the authority of actual angels. As much as they want to believe it, the bottom line is, no one really credible has actually seen him. It must have sounded hollow and ridiculous as they said it out loud, the possibility that Jesus could actually have risen from the dead.

At this point the story takes a twist. This ignorant stranger turns out not to be so ignorant after all. He not only knows all the things that have happened in Jerusalem, he knows why they had to happen: "How foolish you are, and how slow to believe all that the prophets have spoken! Did not the Messiah have to suffer these things and then enter his glory?" Then, as they walk the rest of the six-mile road to Emmaus, "beginning with Moses and all the Prophets" he explains to them "what was said in all the Scriptures concerning himself."

When they reach their destination in Emmaus he seems to be going on. They urge him to stay with them, using the lateness of the hour as their excuse. Really they just want to keep him there. They don't want him to leave because he's raised their hopes. Maybe Jesus' crucifixion was more than just an ignominious end—maybe it was the door to a whole new beginning. But if he's alive, then where is he? Maybe this stranger who seems to know so much can tell them. But there's more to their desire to detain Jesus than a hunger for information—there's something about this man that seems gloriously familiar.

He stays and as they're reclining at the table he takes the bread and breaks it—as if he's the host and not the guest. The moment the bread cracks, the wonderful secret is out. Their eyes are opened and they realize this stranger they've been talking to is the risen Lord Jesus himself, the fully alive victorious Messiah, sitting right there at the table. Then he vanishes and they say to each other, "Were not our hearts burning within us while he talked with us on the road and opened the Scriptures to us?" This stranger had stoked that deep gladness and intense love that only Jesus stokes.

The end. The credits start to roll and we make our way out of the theater back into life with the glow of the story already starting to fade as we face the humdrum, mundane realities of life. Right? Wrong! We don't have to walk out. We're living this story. This episode in Luke tells us how we can stay in the story. We need to be delivered out of the short-sighted way we see life just like those disciples did—and we need it on a regular basis. This little postresurrection vignette shows us the four places where we can find Jesus, where he will meet with us and open our eyes and show us himself. It shows us the four places where Jesus will come to us again and again and shine his light and deliver us out of the dark world of our own erroneous thoughts.

PRAYER

Prayer can sound like a pretty stale word. Most of us could use a fresh way of looking at prayer and that's what this story gives us. We can look at Jesus walking down the road with his disciples and know that prayer is nothing more complicated—and nothing less wonderful—than a real person who's really with us. Jesus was walking beside those two disciples and he's walking beside us too, every step of every day. We're never alone; we never need to do life in isolation from him. He's right here, in communion with us, loving us, helping us, investing himself in our lives. The disciples on the road thought they were alone but they weren't. Even when Jesus disappeared from the range of their vision they weren't alone. Jesus is our Immanuel, our God with us, and now that he's taken on our flesh and entered our realm we will never be alone again.

Sometimes we have trouble connecting the presence of the Lord with the concrete world we live in. We think he's far off in some ethereal realm but he's not. Jesus may be invisible to our physical eyes but he's not a ghost. He made sure the disciples were aware of that fact when he appeared to them later in the upper room after his resurrection. He told them to look at his hands and feet, to go right ahead and touch his body. He asked them for food to eat so they could see him chewing and swallowing real fish. "A ghost does not have flesh and bones, as you see I have." He loves the world he created and he became part of it so he could eat and drink with us. David Wollen, our coworker at Haven, put it like this:

The Almighty gave himself a human face for a reason. Before the incarnation, the words of Isaiah that "as the heavens are higher than the earth so are his ways higher than our ways, and his thoughts than our thoughts" describe what it was like for humanity to relate to God. He was far away and essentially incomprehensible. How do you have a personal relationship with the Incomprehensible?

And so God took on flesh. A human face is something we can understand. Laughter and tears, sitting around a dinner table, being physically tired and needing rest . . . in Jesus, we have a God we can know on a human level. And shockingly, this is a permanent commitment for the second person of the trinity. Jesus will remain clothed in flesh for the rest of eternity with his people. This is how God intends us to know him . . . not just in the future, but now.

Jesus is the God-man, a wondrous union of the glorious transcendent One who created all things and the right here and now Jesus who walks down the road, the soles of his feet keeping pace with ours, who grills fish, and breaks bread, and calls us friends. He's with us now and we can connect with that reality by giving thanks for all the good physical things he gives us. That's what Jesus did—he took bread and as he broke it he gave thanks to his Father. We can give him thanks for small things like Ann Voskamp did. We can notice the sound of a train whistle off in the distance, the flavor of corn on the cob, a whiff of wood smoke floating in the air and be grateful. The Lord made this world and he's giving it to us. We can stop thinking of heaven as somewhere far, far away and realize that this very concrete place we're in is going to be transformed one day. We'll be able to eat and drink with Jesus forever, we'll look at the glory of a re-created physical world with eyes that refract light and ears that vibrate with the waves of sound. This is his world and he has taken on our flesh and blood so he can be in it with us. He reminded the two disciples of that fact when he took the bread and broke it—real physical bread. Our hope is not far away, it's right here, waiting to be transformed.

Not only is he with us, he's engaging us in conversation. He talked to the disciples and he talks to us too. A few years back our son Peter was struck by what he read in Hebrews 13:8: "Jesus Christ is the same yesterday and today and forever." He realized this meant the same Jesus we meet in the gospels is with us right here and now. He hasn't mutated into some remote, unknowable stranger. Edmund Clowney said,

> Jesus Christ, the risen Lord, is the same Jesus who ate with his disciples before his death. The communion that he has with them after his resurrection and ascension has a new and marvelous fullness: it can be extended not only to five hundred brethren at once, but to the countless thousands of those who make up Christ's body to the ends of the earth and the end of time. Yet the fullness of that communion . . . is never less personal than were Christ's dealings with his disciples on earth.[1]

His presence turns our everyday reality into something wondrous. We don't have to strain to get to him; we don't have to figure out where to find him. The same person who walked alongside those two disciples, the same Jesus who came to Levi's party and ate and drank and thoroughly enjoyed their company, tax-collectors though they were, that Jesus is with us—and he's here because he wants to be. Jesus seeks us out because he wants our company. He was born in our flesh, bone of our bone, made like us in every way, except without sin, and then died and rose again—all so we could be together, so we could have a conversation.

Sometimes we think of prayer as a monologue, instigated by us, where we have to wrest our minds away from our everyday thoughts and carry on a one-way conversation with someone who may or may not be listening. Who would want to do that? When we realize that Jesus is taking the initiative just like he did with those two disciples, then the door of our hearts start to open. In fact, Jesus used the analogy of a door when he described prayer in Revelation 3:20. This is his very own description of what prayer is like, the one he wants us to have in our hearts: "Here I am! I stand at the door and knock. If anyone hears my voice and opens the door, I will come in and eat with that person, and they with me."

Jesus wants to talk to the real messy us.

Jesus is telling us that he wants to have a conversation with us. He's knocking at our door, seeking our company, and he's enticing us to open by making a promise: "I will come in and eat with that person, and they with me." Prayer is intimate fellowship with Jesus where we talk together like friends at a meal—or like friends walking down a road. Prayer is a very down to earth conversation with a very real person.

So we're here and Jesus is here. What do we talk about? One of the big problems with prayer is thinking we have to get into a spiritual frame of mind and try to say the things Jesus wants us to say. But if we look at the conversation he had with the two disciples it's obvious that he wants us to get our real thoughts out on the table. "What are you discussing together?" he asks the disciples. He doesn't want a polite conversation like we have with strangers; he wants to enter our real world and hear our real thoughts, even if they're all wrong. It's so easy to fall into formula praying, or launch into a list of requests, or mouth things we don't really mean.

"Jesus calls that hypocrisy," Paul Miller says in his book on prayer. It's "putting on a mask that covers the real you. . . . Ironically, many attempts to teach people to pray encourage the creation of a split personality. You're taught to 'do it right.' Instead of the real messy you meeting God, you try to re-create yourself by becoming spiritual."[2]

Jesus wants to talk to the real messy us. Sometimes we don't even understand why we're restless or anxious or sad, but we can trust in the fact that the Holy Spirit is in us and he knows why. Anyone who's read the Gospels knows that when Jesus comes to dinner he goes right to the heart of people, sometimes asking hard questions that do radical surgery on our status quo. He wants to expose the roots of our fears and unbelief, to bring us out of the dark world of our erroneous thoughts into the light of his wondrously good news—because that's how he re-creates us. He doesn't just promise to handle our problems; he delivers us out of the small world of our immediate concerns and brings us into a more expansive realm. He meets us where we are with all of our dark anti-gospel thoughts and brings us out into the light of reality. We have to make time to meet with him if we want this to happen. If the disciples on the road to Emmaus hadn't met with Jesus, they would have stayed in the dark world of their confusion and unbelief.

Octavius Winslow warns us,

> Guard against the least declension in prayer. Let the first unfavorable symptom that appears alarm you; go to the Lord in your worst

frames; do not stay away from Him until you get a good one. Satan's grand argument to keep a soul from prayer is, "Don't go with that cold and insensible frame, and with that hard and sinful heart; wait until you are more fit to approach God!" Listening to this false reasoning, many poor, distressed, burdened, longing souls have been kept from the throne of grace, and consequently from all comfort and consolation. But . . . Christ says, "Come just as you are."[3]

We need to spend regular time with Jesus, and when we do we can rest assured that it won't be a one-way conversation. Jesus is going to do some talking, not necessarily in an audible voice, as least not in our experience, but he'll respond, he'll communicate and not just to our ears but to our hearts. His Spirit is in us and he's speaking through his Word. He's not some therapist who thinks the cure to everything is a one-way monologue where we get to freely express our feelings. He wants us to do some listening. He will be lovingly honest with us like he was with those disciples. He will bring us out of darkness into the light of truth. "How foolish you are, and how slow to believe all that the prophets have spoken." What the prophets have spoken is very good news for those of us believe—and Jesus wants us to believe it. He gives us loving rebukes designed to bring us out of our unbelief into the deep gladness of who he is and what he's done.

Why are you afraid; why do you doubt; why do you slip back into that unbelieving mindset? Look, it's me, myself, right here with you. Remember how I can multiply bread and fish and turn water into wine and give sight to the blind and raise the dead? See what it means that I died for you, that your sins are forgiven and that you're fully justified and delivered out of that courtroom where you're constantly compelled to make your case. Move out of your self-centered desire to be great and join me in the joy of being a servant. Give up your deadly grown-up self-importance and become a child in my kingdom. Believe that I've been raised from the dead and that you were raised with me. Stop bearing the burden of your own life and turn it over to me. Live in the kingdom I've created through my death and resurrection and be filled with hope in the glorious future that's all yours because you're the sons of God. Believe that I've poured forth the Spirit and that he's in you, preaching good news to your hearts and empowering you to live for my kingdom and my glory.

Believe that I answer prayer.

The two disciples made one request of Jesus—they asked him to stay with them—and he did. Jesus is constantly urging us to believe the very simple but deeply profound truth that if we ask we will receive. Our asking will naturally cover a wide range of subjects, including the very real needs of our here and now existence.

> *"Stay with us," the disciples asked, and he did. Jesus always gives us himself when we ask.*

One day, years ago, Janet needed to get one of the children to a doctor's appointment. She looked high and low for the car keys but couldn't find them anywhere. Eventually she gathered the kids together and asked the Lord to find them. The "amen" was said and no new suggestions came to mind, so she figured she'd better call a locksmith. Lo and behold, what did she find inside the yellow pages but the keys?

We can ask him for simple things like keys. We can ask for deeper, more serious things for ourselves and for other people we love. We might not get the answers we want. We might need to wrestle and we might need to wait, but we'll never have to struggle to get him to listen. The Lord always listens and he always answers. When he does things like helping us find the keys, it reinforces the awesome fact that he's right here with us, fully attentive to everything going on in our lives. It makes us realize all over again how full of love he is and how intensely willing he is to act on our behalf. "Ask, ask, ask," Jesus says, "and you will receive."

"Stay with us," the disciples asked, and he did. Jesus always gives us himself when we ask.

In Revelation 3 the believers in Laodicea had cooled down in their love for Jesus. They thought they were fine but Jesus told them, "You are wretched, miserable, poor, blind and naked" (v. 17). They were living in a delusion of self-sufficiency and Jesus wanted them to know that they were actually in a serious state of need. He wanted them to come to him for what they didn't have in themselves. He wants us to do the same. He wants us to see our desperate need so we will keep on coming to him. We need to build that time into our lives. We need to intentionally answer his knock. We need to talk to him and listen to his answers.

We can tell him how our hearts have been drawn away to idols. We can confess that we have no passion for his kingdom. We can even share the fact that we don't love him like we want to love him. We can just be our real messy selves and freely admit our great insufficiency and ask for his help—he'll gladly provide everything we need.

Jesus said, "I will come in and dine with you and you with me." It's a two-way communion, a give and a take. We not only ask, we receive and give thanks. We offer him our lives from the depths of our hearts in gratitude for his love and for what it compelled him to do. We bow at his feet and tell him how glorious he is and how much we love him. We ask him to show us what he wants us to do. We give him ourselves.

Of course we don't just have communion with the Son, we have communion with the Father. In the Lord's Prayer Jesus teaches us to pray as sons whose greatest desire in life is to see their Father's kingdom come: "Our Father in heaven, hallowed be your name, your kingdom come, your will be done, on earth as it is in heaven." But he also knows the struggles we face living in this world so he tells us to go to the Father and ask him for everything we need. "Give us today our daily bread. Forgive us our debts, as we also have forgiven our debtors. And lead us not into temptation, but deliver us from the evil one." We have communion with the Father because we've been united to the Son and filled with Holy Spirit. Jesus is always opening up that door to us: "In that day you will ask in my name. I am not saying that I will ask the Father on your behalf. No, the Father himself loves you because you have loved me and have believed that I came from God."

THE WORD

Jesus will meet with us just like he met with those two disciples and he will communicate beautiful things to us just like he did to them. Jesus personally opened up the Scriptures to them and he will personally open them up to us. He is a born teacher, born to reveal truth, born as the Word made flesh, the light of the world. Revelation is who he is. He came to teach, to open our eyes, to answer our questions, to expand our minds, to make applications of the good news to our lives. You can see him constantly doing this in the Gospels, calling the people together and speaking his powerful words that are so full of authority they leave shaking their heads in amazement. You can see it in this story of the two disciples, how he opens up the Word and begins to teach them.

Jesus is the great truth-bringer—not just then but now. We can read the Bible knowing he'll be there—explaining, applying, opening up meaning, answering our questions, causing a realization in our hearts through the Spirit. The old original meaning of *realization* is "to make real." The Spirit "realizes" the word in our hearts. He takes the words of the Bible that can seem so detached and irrelevant and makes them real, so we can walk down the road in a new reality just like those two disciples did. The Lord is always in the business of creating junctures between our lives and the Word of God.

Dietrich Bonhoeffer tried to communicate this to his brother-in-law. Rudiger approached the Bible as an expert, armed with all the tools of liberal scholarship that Dietrich knew so well from his studies at the University of Berlin. Dietrich wanted him to understand that there's an entirely different way to read the Bible. He wanted him to know that God actually speaks to us personally through his Word—that we commune with him when we read it. He wrote him a letter to try to explain this:

First of all I will confess quite simply—I believe that the Bible alone is the answer to all our questions and that we need only to ask repeatedly and a little humbly in order to receive this answer. One cannot simply read the Bible like other books. One must be prepared really to enquire of it. Only thus will it reveal itself. Only if we expect from it the ultimate answer shall we receive it. That is because in the Bible God speaks to us. . . . Only if we will venture to enter into the words of the Bible, as though in them this God were speaking to us who loves us and does not will to leave us alone with our questions, only so shall we learn to rejoice in the Bible. . . .

And I would like to tell you now quite personally: since I have learnt to read the Bible in this way—and this has not been for so very long—it becomes every day more wonderful to me. I read it in the morning and evening, often during the day as well, and every day I consider a text which I have chosen for the whole week, and try to sink deeply into it, so as really to hear what it is saying. I know that without this I could not live properly any longer.

If is it I who determine where God is to be found then I shall always find a God who corresponds to me in some way, who is obliging, who is connected with my own nature. But if God determines where he is to be found, then it will be in a place which it is not immediately pleasing to me. . . . This place is the cross of Christ and whoever would find him must go to the foot of the Cross . . . this is the message of the Bible, not only in the New but also in the Old Testament.[4]

That's what Jesus showed the two disciples, that the entire Bible is all about him, from beginning to end, and that the story has always been leading to the cross. As Edmund Clowney says, [the Bible] "is more than a bewildering collection of oracles, proverbs, poems, architectural directions, annals, and prophecies. The Bible has a story line. It traces an unfolding drama."[5]

We need to be continually re-engaging with this great drama. We need to be in the Scriptures; we need to taking in God's Word every day like Bonhoeffer did. We need to be reading the letters of the apostles like they're written personally to us because they are. They were specifically addressed to people living by faith in this final age before Christ returns. Not that the entire Bible isn't ours of course. Paul says even the Old Testament was ultimately meant for those of us upon whom "the ends of the ages has come." From Genesis to Revelation it's all our book. We have the privilege of seeing where the story was headed and how it was fulfilled and where it's taking us in the future. We have the gospel histories of Jesus' living, dying, and being raised again. We have Luke's account of his ascending and then pouring forth the Spirit to create the church.

It's all ours, the Spirit uses it all, but toward the end of the book, between the ascension of Jesus and John's apocalyptic vision, there's this little bundle of letters full of truth on how to live our lives in these in between times. They're not like some old packet of letters hidden in the attic, crumbling with news from times gone by; they're today's mail, addressed to us—to the church awaiting the return of Jesus.

We're the same generation as the early church; we're living in the same time—at the end of the ages. The culture might have changed but the challenge of living life in this final age is fundamentally the same for us as it was for them—it's a matter of living by faith, confident of things hoped for and certain of things not seen. We're called to live by faith and not by sight, and those letters have the power to make the unseen things gloriously real.

We need to be feasting on the Word of God all the time and there's a rich variety of ways we can do it. We can dig in like good students and study it deeply. We can read it quickly from beginning to end to get the sweep of the story. We can read it slowly and devotionally savoring every bite of it like slow food. We can pray through it word by word talking to Jesus as we go, asking him questions, giving him praise. We can listen to preachers and teachers who unfold the Word to us in the light of Christ. If we're preachers and teachers we need to always be doing what Jesus did—always opening the Word and revealing the Christ, always driving toward that necessary crisis when the Messiah would suffer and then enter into his glory. The cross is the crux of the story, the turning point of existence, and it's also the great place of revelation. As Bonhoeffer wrote to his brother-in-law, the cross is the God-appointed meeting place where Jesus can always be found.

THE LORD'S SUPPER

The breaking point in this story comes when Jesus breaks the bread and reveals himself to his disciples. Jesus gave us the Lord's Supper and told us to make it a frequent part of our lives together because it's a powerful place of revelation. In this story, when the bread cracked the two disciples finally recognized Jesus for who he was and it's the same for us. The Lord's Supper is a realizing event. In that crack of the bread and the pouring out of the wine we see Jesus offering himself to us.

The "crack of the bread" is what finally revealed Jesus to our friend Rose Marie Miller. She tells in her book about her deep struggle to connect with Jesus and how one Sunday as she was sitting in a worship service, half listening to her husband preach, it happened. When it came time for communion he raised the loaf of French bread and broke it with a loud crack and that was when she saw it—the spear of the soldiers breaking the body of Christ for her sins. She says, "The fire seemed to have entered my heart, burning away at my intense self-centered moralism."[6]

The crack of the bread and the bloodred wine are Spirit-empowered communicators of Jesus' death on the cross; a death that cracked him open so he could be given to us. He offers us his death and his life like a host at a banquet saying, "Take eat; take drink; this is me given for you." And then we see it—the cross—the Father's plan in all its stunning beauty, the head-shaking resolution of everything, the redemption of our world.

We see it personally, as given to us. It cracks us open and all our "self-centered moralism" is put to death and in the very same crack we see how we are loved. In the cup we see how he pours himself out for us, how we're always needing and not deserving and how he's always loving us in just this way, giving himself and telling us to take and eat, to take and drink, to feast on him. And we do. We take him in, given for us; we take in his life as our own life. It creates a joyous right here and now communion between us—his love giving, our faith taking and giving thanks.

THE FELLOWSHIP

Jesus remade the two disciples; he gave them a revelation of himself, alive from the grave, and they were transformed—but it didn't happen to them in isolation, it happened to them together. Their hearts were bonded with the joy of their shared experience just the way ours are. We're united and reinforced by each other's faith—because Jesus didn't just come to me; he came to you, too. We see Jesus through each other's eyes. Our faith is multiplied by each other's gifts. We're not meant to live this life in isolation; we're meant to live it together. Whenever just two or more of us are gathered, there he is—in the midst of us.

"Didn't our hearts burn within us?" the disciples asked each other. There was something about sharing the experience that made it even more real and glorious to them both. Together they ran seven miles back to Jerusalem in the dark to tell their friends the good news and while they were all gathered together Jesus appeared to them again. It all happened on the first Easter, the very first Sunday gathering of the church. That's where he meets us and pours out his Spirit—when we're gathered together in his name. He meets us and then he sends us out with the message of the gospel.

That's the finale of each and every one of the Easter accounts in the Bible. Jesus comes to where his people are gathered, shows them that he really is alive and then sends them out with the good news. But every sending comes with a promise: "Surely I am with you always, to the very end of the age."

Always.

Notes

1. Edmund Clowney, *Christian Meditation* (Vancouver, BC: Regent College Publishing: 1979), 60.

2. Paul Miller, *A Praying Life* (Colorado Springs: NavPress: 2009), 33.

3. Octavius Winslow, *Evening Thoughts* (Grand Rapids: Reformation Heritage Books: 2003), 543.

4. Eric Metaxis, *Bonhoeffer: Pastor, Martyr, Prophet, Spy* (Nashville: Thomas Nelson, 2010), 136–37.

5. Edmund Clowney, *The Unfolding Mystery* (Phillipsburg, NJ: P&R Publishing, 1988), 11.

6. Rose Marie Miller, *From Fear to Freedom* (Colorado Springs: WaterBrook Press, 1994), 69.

The End—
and the Beginning

You can never get too much of Jesus. Every other sun will dim; every other center will lose its pull; every other resource will dry up—but not Jesus. He just keeps getting bigger and better.

Writing this book has made us realize just how glorious and inexhaustible he really is and how un-centered and empty life is when we miss him. When we started writing we asked our friends to pray for the Spirit to enlarge our hearts so we could somehow grasp his glory and communicate it to you. Our prayer as we wrote has been for you, that Jesus would enlarge your heart along with ours. Now we've reached the end of the book and the surface has barely been scratched—but that's okay. As believers we're always heading toward more of Jesus.

When our daughter Kate was five, she and her friend Becca loved the musical *Annie*. Not only did they know all the songs, they could recite practically every word of the script. If you've seen the movie you know that Little Orphan Annie was a spark plug who livened things up wherever she went. When Daddy Warbucks decided he was going to adopt her, his house staff could barely suppress their joy. Every time they passed each other they whispered the news: "We've got Annie."

Well, we've got Jesus. We're got the all-glorious Son of God. Let's keep whispering the news to each other so none of us will miss him. Everything he is, everything he's done, everything he possesses, all belongs to us. He's right here with us in this moment, pouring out grace upon grace, and up ahead is that glorious day when we'll finally see him face to face.

We've got Jesus and he's got us. Our prayer as we close this book is that the Spirit of Christ would fill us all with the joy of that realization.

Acknowledgments

It's good to be able to close by expressing our thanks to the One who is worthy. Thank you, Lord Jesus, for all the people you orchestrated into our lives and made a part of this book. Thank you for our daughter, Kate, and our son, Peter, and all the friends who freely allowed us to tell their stories. Thank you for our mutual faith in you.

Thank you for Moody Publishers and their genuine commitment to bringing you glory and building up the body of Christ. Thank you for Greg Thornton who said, "This book is a bull's-eye for us," and for Duane Sherman who brings a pastor's heart to publishing and prayed at our dining room table that "every word would be written in trust." Thank you for Betsey Newenhuyse who identified with much of the manuscript and made it live, and for Erik Peterson who visually captured the concept, and for everyone else who is part of the process.

Thank you for the board of directors of Haven Ministries and for Jim Sanders at Ambassador Advertising Agency, who insisted that this book be written. Thank you for David Wollen and his invaluable contributions to both the concept and the content of the book. Thank you for the joy of seeing his transforming response to the gospel over the years. Thank you for Adrian Crum, Corum Hughes, and Troy Lamberth for their long-suffering support of Charles.

Thank you for Sally Lloyd-Jones who told Janet to just "listen to the Lord" as she wrote. Thank you for Ted Hamilton, Darrell Johnson, and Jack Miller, who have passionately preached Jesus into our hearts.

Thank you for all the friends who faithfully prayed for us: Linda, Kate, Helen, Vicki, Lisa, Cyndi, Dianna, Kathleen, Jessie, Cate, Nancy, David, Adrian, Donald—and all the others.

Finally, Lord, thank you for yourself. Words fail.

Charles and Janet Morris serve with Haven Ministries (haventoday.org), which broadcasts HAVEN Today to more than 600 stations in the United States and Canada and on multiple outlets internationally. The half-hour program, a 60-second program and weekly commentary can be heard on the Moody Radio Network, as well as Moody owned-and-operated stations. The ministry also publishes in both print and on-line a daily devotional called "Anchor".